T0004136

LOOK UP LONDON

Katie Wignall

LOOK UP LONDON

Discover the
details you
have never
noticed before
in 10 walks

greenfinch

CONTENTS

Introduction

I cannot recall the exact moment at which I thought of Look Up London, but I vividly remember walking along Oxford Street with a friend and discussing ways to share with others the quirks of the capital that hide above the eye line. I showed my friend a little beaver, teetering on top of a building, clutching an 'H'. I explained that the poor little guy is a reminder of a hat manufacturer on this site from the 19th century, the H standing for Henry Heath's company and the beaver because his skin was used for the felt of top hats. He didn't seem to be aware that his days were numbered. The beaver, not the friend.

In 2015, after a few years of posting images and the history behind them on Twitter and Tumblr, I was made redundant from my job in marketing and was considering ways in which to make talking about London history a full-time career.

I applied for the Blue Badge Tourist Guide course, an intense two-year training programme and the UK's top accreditation for guiding. After passing 11 exams and gaining the award for 'best overall presentations', I found the things I enjoyed most were the esoteric details, discovering little-known facts that most born-and-bred Londoners (like myself) are not aware of.

I continued with Look Up London throughout the course, posting a new blog about the city's quirky history each week – a selection of the most unusual clocks, for example, a favourite being the eye-shaped model protruding from Moorfields Eye Hospital. I also began to run walking tours for the public (admittedly it was a few months before anyone other than friends and family booked!). But fast-forward to today and I have a regular weekend programme with more than 10 different public walks that tend to sell out.

It is an amazing privilege to take first-time visitors around London's major sights. You appreciate the wondrous Tower of London or Westminster Abbey through their eyes, seeing the sites afresh, and I am so proud to share this city's story. But I also love showing Londoners the little alleys, tiny details and, above all, the amazing history hiding in plain sight.

This all changed in 2020. As the borders closed and we were instructed to stay at home, I knew there had to be a way to continue sharing London's history. I turned to virtual tours, sharing images and video footage while sitting at home and explaining their significance online to hundreds of people across

the world. I was delighted to be able to reach new enthusiasts who wanted to explore London with me. I have been so touched by the messages people send me saying how much the tours helped them at this difficult time, but the truth is I needed to continue doing what I love just as much.

Look Up London is about that exhilarating feeling of discovering something for the first time. Perhaps you literally look up and spot a plaque or sculpture you've never seen before, or maybe it's a roundel embedded in the pavement that piques your interest.

My aim and passion is to share the amazing stories that often go unnoticed in this city, so whether it's your first time visiting or you've lived here your whole life, I want you to be curious and feel that excitement through Look Up London, the book.

Left (top) Moorfields Eye Hospital clock; **(bottom)** Henry Heath Beaver

Walking London

Walking is without doubt the best way to discover London. The slower pace gives you a chance to soak in the architecture and street names, and to ponder the people that have walked this path before you.

In planning this book, just as when I'm planning walking tours in real life, the biggest challenge was choosing what to leave out. The 10 areas I've chosen for walks arose from a desire to map out routes that stood apart from my Look Up London public walks, giving me the chance to get inspired by new stories and sharing the diversity of London's history and architecture. It also meant that, for the wonderful (and committed!) people who have joined all of my walking tours, there is now much more to discover.

With each walk, one aim is to follow the key guiding principle of the TVP (top visual priority) – that is, what is so visually striking that you simply have to explain its existence. But another aim is to guide you towards the less-trodden paths and down the streets in search of little details you might otherwise miss.

As ever, the choice as to which stories to include is a personal one. I like sharing the stories of unsung heroes alongside the household names. You may feel on some walks that I've 'left out' a major bit of history, but that's the wonderful thing about London's past. There's always more to add and discover!

The text for the walks endeavours to make the routes as easy to follow as possible, so coupled with the maps I hope the walks can be easily navigated. That being said, it's impossible to fit all the street names in one map image so you might find it helpful to have an A–Z with you or to use Google Maps for back up (see page 216 for links).

I truly hope that you feel inspired and excited while out and about on these walks and I'd love for you to share your pictures with me online. Or maybe if you spot something else en route then ask me a question. If you've been on a walking tour with me in person you will know that I adore questions!

You can tag me on Instagram and Twitter @look_uplondon, TikTok @lookuplondon and Facebook @lookuplondonwalks.

Opposite Figure from *Dr Salter's Daydream*, Bermondsey

Using this book

This book features 10 London walks, each focused on a different area in the capital. Interspersed among the walks, a selection of Top 10 and In Focus features offer a deeper delve into what the city has to offer.

Each walk is accompanied by a map of the route, with selected sites numbered. To help navigate the route, the numbers also appear in the text that follows. On page 216, you can find links to the routes on Google Maps.

Each walk offers an engaging tour of the area in question, revealing little-known and quirky facts about the sites on the map and other points of interest along the way.

From historic pubs to green spaces and from unusual museums to statues and independent cafes, each of these pages list 10 of my London favourites.

In Focus pages look at features of the city that tend to go unnoticed: blue plaques, boundary markers, fire insurance marks, communication infrastructure and street furniture.

Top 10 moments that shaped London

In around 2,000 years of recorded history, several key moments have left lasting marks on the capital. Here are 10 of the most significant events.

57 AD
Roman Emperor Claudius invaded England in 43 AD. The Romans chose a location on the banks of the River Thames – close to today's London Bridge – and established a trading port. Londinium, as it became known, had another river flowing through it at the time: the River Walbrook. This has since been covered over, but is remembered in a street name. Close by you can now find the London Mithraeum (see page 77), a museum on the site of a former Roman temple. The museum holds the earliest recorded financial transaction in London, from 57 AD, which describes the money owed between two Roman citizens. It marks the start of the City as an international centre of finance.

886 AD ❶
After the Romans left Londinium in 410 AD, the city would not be inhabited again for more than 400 years. By tradition, King Alfred the Great (r. c.886–99) re-established London in 886, landing at Queenhithe. Pictured here, an epic 30-m (100-ft) long mosaic at Queenhithe Dock, EC4, tells

the City's story. In the meantime, while the Roman city crumbled into ruins, another settlement was growing. The Anglo-Saxons chose to establish a town outside the Roman walls, in an area close to today's Covent Garden.

1534 ❷

King Henry VIII (r. 1509–47) had a problem. He was married to the powerful, Spanish, Catherine of Aragon but did not believe she could give him a male heir and the Pope would not grant him a divorce. Circumventing the Pope's authority, the Act of Supremacy was passed, declaring King Henry VIII the Supreme Head of the Church, not the Pope. This set in motion further acts breaking up the major religious houses of London, including Bermondsey Abbey, the Charterhouse and Blackfriars Monastery (the site of which is now occupied by The Blackfriar pub, pictured; see also, page 37).

1666 ❸

In the early hours of 2 September 1666, a fire started in Thomas Farriner's bakery on Pudding Lane. By the time the Great Fire of London had finally been extinguished on 5 September, 87 churches, 44 livery halls and 13,200 homes had been destroyed and new building regulations changed

the appearance of London forever. Pictured here is Monument, erected in commemoration of the event (see also, page 28).

1858 ❹

During an extraordinarily hot summer, the River Thames began to smell. It was full of human waste, thanks to newly introduced flushing toilets, and residents were unable to cope. With the new Houses of Parliament directly on the river, members of parliament could not ignore the so-called 'Great

Stink'. An act for building London's new sewer system was passed into law on 2 August and the Metropolitan Board of Works, under the direction of Joseph Bazalgette started work on an infrastructure project that would create the embankment (pictured), reclaiming around 22 acres of land from the river.

1863 ⑤

On 10 January 1863, the world's first underground railway opened. The Metropolitan Railway ran between Paddington (called Bishop's Road at the time) and Farringdon Street. On its first day the railway carried 38,000 passengers. Today, an average of two million people use the Tube every day.

1899

The London Government Act of 1899 revolutionized the administration of the capital. It created 28 metropolitan boroughs, replacing a haphazard parish system and leading to grand town hall buildings for each new borough. In 1963 another act would create Greater London, giving us the 32 London boroughs we have today.

1937 ⑥

When the Faraday building in Blackfriars was extended in the early 1930s, its new bulk partially blocked

6

7

the view of St Paul's Cathedral from the River Thames. In 1937 the City of London Corporation initiated a policy known as St Paul's Heights, protecting views of the dome from key locations across London. When you look at the curious shapes of London's skyscrapers – among them the triangular Leadenhall Building (aka the Cheesegrater, seen to the left in this photo) – it is because they are adhering to these protected views.

1940 ❼

On 25 August 1940, during the Second World War, the first bomb fell on the City of London and a plaque on Fore Street marks the site (pictured). From 7 September 1940, and for 57 consecutive days and nights, London would suffer through The Blitz, which killed an estimated 30,000 Londoners and destroyed more than one million London homes.

2000

On 4 May 2000, Ken Livingstone became the first Mayor of London. The mayor is the head of the Greater London Authority and responsible for the £17 billion budget for the city, setting policies for transport, police, housing, planning and arts and culture across London.

Top 10 architectural styles

London's architecture varies tremendously. It is one of the things that makes the city so visually exciting. Here are some general pointers to help identify what you are looking at.

Norman ❶
Arriving with the Norman Conquest that started in 1066, this 11th-century style is typified by huge, thick columns and bold, stylized stonework. Good examples can be found in St Bartholomew the Great and St John's Chapel within the Tower of London.

Gothic ❷
Popular in Europe from the 1200s–1500s, this style is all about light and height. Delicate columns support tall, pointed arches, while flying buttresses provide support from the outside like a rib cage. This allows the walls to include stained-glass windows that flood the interior with light. The style is often used for cathedrals, and Westminster Abbey is a fine example, with the highest Gothic vaulted ceiling in the country, at 31m (102ft).

Classical ❸
Inspired by travel across Italy, Inigo Jones created the first classical building in England in Queen's House, Greenwich, in 1636. Influenced by the architecture of ancient Greece

and Rome, the style is typified by harmonious proportions, symmetry and the use of orders. There are five different classical orders, defined by the type of column and capital.

English Baroque ❹

Take the flamboyance of Italian baroque – dramatic curves and the play of light and shade – but calm it down a bit and you have the restrained grandeur of St Paul's Cathedral by Sir Christopher Wren. English baroque contains classical elements such as orders and balanced compositions, and is mostly associated with Wren's work in London. It was a relatively short-lived style, lasting from 1666 until the early 1700s.

The Georgian House ❺

The Building Act of 1774 aimed to standardize housing to protect against fire. It listed four types of house, called 'rates', as determined by size and value. The best example of a surviving 'first' rate house can be found in Bedford Square, Bloomsbury. It has steps leading up to the front door and its largest windows appear on the first floor – the piano nobile – generally being taller than they are wide. Storeys grow progressively smaller on the upper floors of the house and might culminate in a sloped attic.

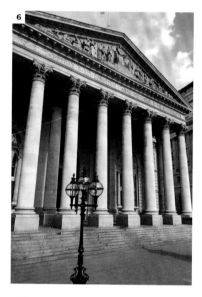

Neoclassical 6

As the British Empire grew during the late 18th and early 19th centuries, an architectural style for grand civic buildings emerged that combined simple forms on a grand scale with a nod to the former empire of Rome. If you think of the architecture of libraries, banks and museums, they are usually in this style.

Neo-Gothic 7

A rival to neoclassical, neo-Gothic style (also Gothic revival or Victorian Gothic) was an attempt to celebrate a more 'English' architectural style, looking back to the medieval period and the golden age of cathedral building. A good example of the style in London is St Pancras Station. The style incorporates the pointed arches and vertical emphasis of Gothic but with extravagant embellishments that leave no surface free of flourish and are often rendered in bright colours.

Art Deco 8

From the French *arts décoratifs*, this style swept through London in the early 20th century and is mostly associated with cinemas and entertainment venues. However, one of the best-known examples is the *Daily Telegraph* building on Fleet Street, which is identifiable by its emphasis on simple, bold shapes and colour, exuding glamour.

Brutalist ❾

From the French *béton brut* meaning 'raw concrete', this mid-20th-century style tends to divide opinion. Hulking mass, exaggerated shapes and a general feeling of 'heaviness' are coupled with the use of cast concrete. A good example is the Barbican housing estate in the City of London.

Postmodern ❿

Emerging from the late 1970s, postmodernism was a reaction against the strict forms of modernism that had prevailed from the 1930s to the 1960s. Postmodernist architects took forms and theories from early architectural styles but added whimsy and colour to their designs. Within postmodernism are branches of other styles, such as high-tech, where buildings unashamedly show you what materials they are made of and how they are put together. A famous example of this is Lloyd's of London's 'inside-out' headquarters on Lime Street.

The
walks

City of London walk

START
Tower Hill London
Underground Station

FINISH
1 New Change,
EC4M 9AF

DISTANCE
3.3km (2 miles)

The City is unlike anywhere else in the capital. It is one of the most important financial markets in the world as well as an ancient walled city with a history spanning two millennia. As the oldest part of London, it retains many unique quirks and privileges that you shall discover along the walk. Today we know it mainly as a centre of finance, but for around 1,600 years of London's history the City *was* London.

Often referred to as the Square Mile, the City was founded around 2,000 years ago by the Romans, intended as a trading port and town. In time it gained an enclosing wall – a large section is still visible outside Tower Hill Station – and despite being ravaged by plague, fire and bombs, it has always bounced back stronger.

Opposite The Tower of London

The walk begins at Tower Hill Station ❶ **When you exit the Tube, head up the nearby steps for a view over the Tower of London.**

The tower in the name is the White Tower, which sits at the centre of the walled complex. It has a turret on each corner, topped with onion-shaped domes and golden weathervanes. Built in the 1080s, the Tower of London has been used as a royal palace, a military fortress, a prison and even a zoo! Today it is one of London's top tourist attractions, with crowds flocking to see the Crown Jewels.

Turning away from the tower, take some time to admire the large sundial artwork by John Chitty and Edwin Russell, unveiled in 1992. Panels encircling the base depict moments in London's history from the Roman occupation to the present day.

Go back down the steps and follow the map along Trinity Square, turning right under the entrance to Leonardo Royal Hotel. Ahead you will see one of the best surviving fragments of London's Roman Wall ❷ You can walk through the wall here, to appreciate its thickness and how impressive it would have been when first built. The Romans built the wall around 120 AD, having established the city of Londinium around 43 AD. No one is sure why the wall was built,

possibly for defence, but more likely for tax reasons, as it enabled officials to charge merchants to import goods into the City. The walls have been altered and added to many times over the centuries. You can identify the true Roman sections by the lines of red tiles near the base of the wall.

Retrace your steps back towards Tower Hill Station, passing a neat little building on your right. Designed by Samuel Wyatt in the 1790s, this is Trinity House, the headquarters of the charity of the same name. Given a royal charter in 1514, the charity ensures the safety of shipping and seafarers around the United Kingdom. Throughout its history, the City relied on the Thames and shipping for its wealth. If you look up at the chunky stone white building next to Trinity House, you will spot the statue of a very muscly Father Thames astride an anchor and gesturing out to the East. Built in 1922, this is the former Port of London Authority (PLA) headquarters. The building is now a Four Seasons hotel, but the PLA still manages the length of the tidal Thames – around 155km (95 miles) of river.

Cross inside Trinity Square Gardens. Within this green space stands the Tower Hill Memorial, two monuments to civilian merchant sailors who died during the First and

Second World Wars. But there is also another memorial here. **Make your way towards the cluster of palm trees and the former site of the Tower Hill Scaffold.** Between the 14th and 18th centuries, criminals and traitors were executed in front of large crowds on Tower Hill. Some of the more famous names are remembered on panels on the ground, including James, Duke of Monmouth, who had the misfortune of enduring seven blows of the axe before he eventually died, in 1685.

Following the map, leave the gardens and cross over the road towards the Tower of London. Then turn right and walk towards All Hallows by the Tower church on Byward Street ❸ As you approach the church, there are two interesting things to look out for. The first is a small, white tombstone-shaped bollard embedded in the pavement. This is a Tower of London Liberty boundary marker. It is one of 22 surviving markers that denote land owned by the Board of Ordnance, a military government department founded in the 16th century, which had its headquarters in the Tower of London. It later became the War Department, hence the 'WD' you can see on the boundary marker; the Board of Ordnance's symbol is the broad arrow at the top. Secondly, atop a black pillar is a sculpture of a silver and red dragon, the traditional symbol and guardian of the City of London; it lets you know you have now entered the City proper.

Although extensively rebuilt after the Second World War, All Hallows by the Tower is one of the oldest churches in London. If you get a chance to look inside, you can find the only standing piece of Saxon stonework in its original position, thought to date from the 7th century.

Continue on Byward Street, crossing the road at the Hung, Drawn and Quartered pub on the corner of Great Tower Street. On the side of the pub is a plaque recalling a quote from Samuel Pepys, a naval administrator who lived nearby and whose famous diary from the 17th century gives us a great insight into life in London at that time. Pepys had gone to witness the public execution of Major-General Harrison – found guilty of regicide – on 13 October 1660, which did not in fact take place on Tower Hill, but at Charing Cross. Pepys quips that Harrison looked 'as cheerful as any man could do in that condition. He was presently cut down, and his head and heart shown to the people, at which there were great shouts of joy.'

All Hallows by the Tower was first mentioned in the Domesday Book in 1086, but may be far older (a plaque outside claims 675 AD).

Walk along Great Tower Street then turn left onto St Dunstan's Hill, which flanks St Dunstan in the East Church Garden ❹ Opened in 1971, this is one of the most enchanting gardens in the City. It is home to the ruins of St Dunstan in the East, a medieval church, rebuilt in the 18th century, that was then gutted by bombs during the Second World War and never rebuilt. Today there are still more than 50 places of worship within the City of London, but there used to be many more. Incredibly the City also boasts over 350 green and open spaces (although some are *tiny*). Many of these gardens are former churchyards, closed for burials in the 19th century as London's population

Opposite (top) Dragon boundary marker;
(bottom) St Dunstan's in the East

skyrocketed. **Exit through the ruins onto St Dunstan's Lane, arriving at St Mary at Hill.** Another of the City's churches, St Mary at Hill was rebuilt by Christopher Wren in 1674, following the Great Fire of London.

Continue left, pausing to admire Watermen's Hall ❺ This is the headquarters of one of the City's 110 livery companies. First established as trade guilds in medieval times, these companies grouped together to establish prices, ensure standards and control who could enter the profession. Although the river had provided jobs since Roman times, The Company of Watermen and Lightermen first received official acknowledgement in an act of Parliament from 1514. The hall dates from the late 18th century.

Walk to the end of St Mary at Hill, turning right onto Lower Thames Street. Across the road is the former Billingsgate Fish Market, probably the site of a market since Roman times but made official by royal charter from 1327. Originally a general market, it started to specialize in fish from the 16th century. The building dates from 1876 but the market moved out in 1982 and is now found by Canary Wharf.

Follow the map up Monument Street towards the Monument ❻ Completed in 1676, designed by

Christopher Wren and Robert Hooke, and with a height of 61.5m (202ft), this is the tallest isolated stone column in the world and 10m (39ft) taller than Nelson's Column in Trafalgar Square! It commemorates the Great Fire of London in 1666, which started very near here, on Pudding Lane. At around 1am on 2 September, a rogue spark leapt from the oven of Thomas Farriner's bakery, starting a fire that lasted four days and destroyed 80 per cent of the City of London. Walk around the Monument to appreciate the wonderful stone carving of Caius Gabriel Cibber, sculptor of choice for many of Wren's London projects. Look out for a witch-like figure depicting envy. She personifies the fire and creeps back under the gutter, sucking in her flames.

From the Monument, walk up Pudding Lane and turn right onto Eastcheap. Cross the road and turn left into Philpot Lane. Keep your eyes peeled on the corner building to spot one of London's smallest public sculptures; two mice with a piece of cheese ❼ Built in 1860 as offices and warehouses, the story goes that while this building was under construction, two workers got into an argument over one stealing the other's cheese sandwich. It escalated into a fight and one of the men fell to his death. To add

to the irony, the sandwich was later found nibbled by a mouse. Whether or not there is any truth to this story, it is still a fun little oddity to look out for.

At the top of Philpot Lane, cross Fenchurch Street and continue on Lime Street. Turn left into Lime Street Passage and into Leadenhall Market ❽ Designed by Horace Jones and finished in 1881, this was a poultry market (menacing-looking black hooks for stringing up birds still hang above the shop signs). The name comes from a 14th-century lead-roofed manor house that once stood on this site but – as ever in the City – the history goes back further. If it is open, pop into Nicholson & Griffin hairdressers on the corner and ask nicely to see their Roman ruins ❾ Head down the stairs and in the basement you can see a small section of the Roman basilica. This was part of a complex of civic buildings built in the 1st century AD that housed law courts, the town hall and a market.

Follow the map to exit Leadenhall on Gracechurch Street. Turn right and left into Cornhill. After a short walk, look up to spy the Cornhill Devils peering down at you ❿ The building (54–55 Cornhill) was designed by Ernest Runtz in 1893. During construction, there was supposedly an argument over planning permission

Right (top) Carved figure at the Monument; **(centre)** Leadenhall Market; **(bottom)** Lombard Street

with the next-door neighbour, the vicar of St Peter Upon Cornhill Church. Runtz is said to have added these devils to spite the vicar.

Take the next left into St Michael's Alley. Immediately facing you between the buildings is the facade of St Michael Cornhill ⑪ The network of alleys here really gives you the impression that you have stepped back in time, and you get a true sense of the scale and density of the old City of London.

It was in the churchyard of St Michael Cornhill that, in 1852, a man called Pasqua Rosée introduced coffee to London for the first time. Rosée was assistant to the merchant Daniel Edwards, who traded with the Middle East and helped Rosée establish a stall here in 1652. Early coffee would have tasted disgusting to our modern standards; bitter and gritty, it was compared to 'soot' and 'dirt'. However, thanks to its invigorating and addictive properties (and a fair bit of marketing spin about health benefits), it became hugely popular; by 1663 there were 83 coffeehouses in the City.

Today, the Jamaica Wine House stands on the site of the Jamaica Coffeehouse. Typically, each coffeehouse attracted a particular type of merchant and this one was popular with West Indian traders. Among the wealthiest of all City merchants in the 18th century, they made their money importing rum, tobacco and, above all, sugar from slave plantations.

Explore the alleys here to see two traditional London restaurants: the George & Vulture (rebuilt 1748) and, ducking into Bull Court (off Castle Court), the atmospheric Simpson's Tavern ⓬ Established in 1723 by Thomas Simpson in Billingsgate, Simpson's cooked fish for workers who brought in their catch. The restaurant moved to its current location in 1757 and has been here ever since. Though it dates from the late 18th century, it has a c.1900 shopfront.

Retrace your steps to exit the alley onto Birchin Lane, turn left and then right onto Lombard Street. The street takes its name from the Italian financiers who settled in the area from the 14th century. Look up to see some of the restored hanging signs that would once have crowded the street. One of the most impressive is the golden grasshopper, family symbol of Thomas Gresham, a 16th-century merchant who had a goldsmith at no. 68. He would go on to found the Royal Exchange, which you shall see shortly.

Also on Lombard Street, on the site of nos 5–10 ⓭ stood Lloyd's Coffeehouse from 1691–1785, established by Edward Lloyd for seafaring men. Merchants would gather at his establishment to swap insider knowledge and make business deals. Over time, groups of merchants started a practice of pooling their money together to share the financial risk of a long sea voyage and would write their names on a piece of paper to agree the contract. Hence the term 'underwriting' and the development of the insurance industry. Today Lloyd's is the world's specialist insurance and reinsurance market.

Continue along Lombard Street until you reach St Mary Woolnoth on the corner ⓮ Completed in 1727, to the designs of Nicholas Hawksmoor, with its heavy-set stone facade and squat twin towers, it is one of the more unusual looking churches in the City. In 1780 the rector here was John Newton, a former captain of slave ships who renounced the trade and became an advocate of the abolition movement. In 1772 he wrote the words for 'Amazing Grace', later made into a hymn, that references his religious epiphany: 'I once was lost, but now am found, Was blind but now I see.'

Turn right off Lombard Street and walk through Pope's Head Alley. Its name probably refers to the hanging sign of a 15th-century tavern that once stood here. Look up along

the alley to spot a modern carving of a Pope's head. **You now emerge into Bank Junction, the financial heart of the City.** Towards the right-hand side is the Royal Exchange **15** Now a luxury shopping arcade, this is the third Royal Exchange building on the site. The original was a merchant trading hub, established by Thomas Gresham in 1571. Colourful clocks hanging off each side of the building show representations of the earlier Royal Exchanges. Look up to spot the golden grasshopper weathervane that sits atop the dome at the east end.

On the other side of the forecourt is the Bank of England **16** Established in 1694 to act as banker for the government, today it is the United Kingdom's central bank. It has a rather good free museum that is worth visiting if you have time. Take a closer look at the black lampposts that surround this public space. There are 12 in total, and each displays the name and golden coat of arms of one of the livery companies mentioned earlier. Throughout the centuries, these companies have squabbled among themselves, fighting for privileges, with occasional resorts to violence. To remedy this, in 1515 the Lord Mayor established an Order of Precedence to rank the companies by wealth and prestige. It is the top 12 of these – known as 'the great 12' – that feature on the lampposts here.

Opposite The Royal Exchange at Bank Junction **Right** No. 1 Poultry

Follow the map to exit Bank Junction and head up Poultry. On your left you will see a darker stone building with fluted columns and blue railings at its base ⑰ This is Mansion House, official home to the Lord Mayor of the City of London. The first Lord Mayor was Henry Fitzailwyn, appointed in 1189, and who served for life until 1212. It is one of the oldest continuously held civic offices in the world. Today the Lord Mayor typically serves for one year and is unpaid, acting as an ambassador for the City and leader of its governing body, the City of London Corporation. Mansion House was completed in 1752 by George Dance the Elder. Look up at the triangular pediment, and you can see a personification of the City as a woman trampling across evil, while trade and the arts flourish around her.

Continue up Poultry, which turns into Cheapside. 'Cheap' is an Old English word meaning 'market' or 'trading place' and this is essentially the City's high street. Narrower streets branching off it (Bread Street, Milk Street) are like supermarket aisles showing us what was once for sale. One of the widest streets in the City, Cheapside often hosted ceremonial and royal processions. If you look up at No.1 Poultry you can see carved panels reflecting this history ⑱ They were

saved from a demolished 19th-century building that once stood on this site.

Turn right onto Ironmonger Lane which, perhaps unsurprisingly, was the former site of ironmongers who were based here from the 12th to mid-15th centuries. On the corner, look up and you will see a figure in bronze ⑲ This is Thomas Becket, born here c.1120, who would rise through the ranks of the Court and Church to become the Archbishop of Canterbury. In 1170, supposedly on the order of King Henry II (r. 1154–89), he was brutally murdered by four knights in his own cathedral. The site of his martyrdom quickly became a popular place of pilgrimage and he was canonized in 1173.

A little further up Ironmonger Lane, another bronze figure graces the wall, but this time of a woman ⑳ This is a Mercers' Maiden, symbol of the Mercers' Company, which ranks highest of all the aforementioned livery companies. Given a royal charter in 1394, the Mercers historically traded luxurious cloth but today manage a lucrative property portfolio and give millions to charity. This particular maiden marks the site of their hall, but Mercers' Maidens feature wherever they own property in London.

Continue on Ironmonger Lane, turning left onto Gresham Street – named after the Thomas you met earlier – and crossing the road to enter Guildhall Yard ㉑ This is the heart of the City of London Corporation, the body that governs the City of London today. An ancient place of decision-making, Guildhall was first built in 1411 but has been substantially altered over the centuries. The white front porch dates from the 18th century and the roof was rebuilt following bomb damage from the Second World War.

Today Guildhall hosts banquets, ceremonies and is where the annual Lord Mayor's Show starts, a procession involving the newly elected Lord Mayor 'showing' himself or herself (there have been two

female Lord Mayors) to the public. But look down at the floor to see a black line curving around the yard. This marks out an even earlier building, London's Roman Amphitheatre. Built in the 1st century AD with a capacity of 7,000, its ruins in the basement of the Guildhall Art Gallery are open to the public, free of charge.

To the left of Guildhall is the brutalist office building of the City of London Corporation. The curious grey section on stilts hosts the boardroom used by the Court of Aldermen, 25 of whom are elected by City residents and workers to represent them. This electorate, unique in the country for including business workers, also votes for the 100 Common Councillors who, with the Aldermen, make up the Court of Common Council. The court manages the day-to-day running and ceremonial events of the City.

The last building within Guildhall Yard is St Lawrence Jewry. The official church of the City of London Corporation, it was rebuilt after the Great Fire of London by Christopher Wren in 1677 and further restored after bomb damage in 1957 by Cecil Brown. Look to the very top of the steeple to see a strangely shaped weathervane. This is a gridiron to remember the fact that poor St Lawrence was barbecued

Left Guildhall Yard

to death as a Christian martyr in 3rd-century Rome.

Leave Guildhall and continue along Gresham Street. At the corner of Wood Street look right to admire the lone tower of the former St Alban's Wood Street ㉒ Another of Christopher Wren's churches, it was not rebuilt after damage during the Second World War and is now a private home and office.

Turn left down Wood Street and on towards Cheapside. Near the end of the street is a small garden with a towering plane tree ㉓ This is the former churchyard of St Peter Cheap (a reference to the street rather than Peter's generosity), which was not rebuilt after it was destroyed in the

Great Fire of London. It is thanks to the preservation order on this tree – which some claim was planted in the 17th century – that these small shops on Cheapside survive. The tree cannot be removed and replaced with a larger development. There are records of shops here as far back as 1401, but those you can see today date from the 17th century with 19th and 20th century frontages.

Across Cheapside is a far newer building, One New Change by Jean Nouvelle, which opened in 2010. It represents the City's efforts to attract visitors outside of the Monday–Friday working week, and is handy for its selection of restaurants and free toilets in the basement. If you have time you may want to head up to the free public rooftop, which has a spectacular view of St Paul's Cathedral. You may also want to visit inside St Paul's, which is typically open for sightseeing every day except Sundays. Although there is free access for private prayer in a side chapel, tickets can be purchased to see the rest of the cathedral and climb the dome.

TOP 10 · HISTORIC PUBS

*Never just simply a place for a drink, here are 10 favourite pubs
with history, atmosphere and the occasional tall tale!*

1. Ye Olde Cheshire Cheese, Fleet Street
Rebuilt in 1667, this gem is a maze of cosy and atmospheric rooms, especially the cellars in the basement. Look out for Polly, the stuffed grey African parrot who once entertained the journalists and lawyers who flocked to this pub.

2. The Angel, Rotherhithe
The current pub dates from the 1830s but might incorporate parts of an earlier pub that stood here from the 17th century. In any case, it's a perfect spot to enjoy some of the best riverside views back over central London.

3. Holly Bush, Hampstead
First built in 1643, as stables for the fancier homes nearby, this was rebuilt in 1797 by the painter George Romney and then converted into a pub in 1807.

4. Seven Stars, Holborn
Although the painted frontage declares 1602, some argue the building more likely appeared after the 1680s. It is still very old and packed with character, mainly thanks to the landlady, Roxy Beaujolais.

5. The Dove, Hammersmith
Another charming riverside pub, The Dove holds the Guinness World Record for the smallest bar in the United Kingdom. A coffeehouse from the 1600s originally, it was rebuilt in the 1700s.

6. Ye Olde Mitre, Holborn
It might take you a few tries just to find this pub down a narrow alley off Hatton Garden.

Rebuilt in 1773 (although the sign says est. 1546), it's tempting to believe Elizabeth I really did once dance around a tree here when it was a garden.

7. Prospect of Whitby, Wapping
Established in 1520, this is one of London's oldest riverside pubs. Peer over the side and you'll glimpse the replica hangman's noose, a gruesome reminder of the fate that awaited caught pirates and thieves. Thankfully you can relax and enjoy the 18th- and 19th-century surroundings.

8. The Blackfriar
Although it's not that old – remodelled in the early 1900s – this is a unique little pub with a staggering interior that sits on the site of the Blackfriars monastery, founded in the 13th century.

9. Old Doctor Butler's Head
The pub might only be 19th century, but its namesake is a curious figure who, in 1603, came to fame by reviving a comatose priest by encasing his body in a slaughtered cow. This 'doctor' went on to set up a franchise of medicinal ale, apparently sold on this site.

10. The George, Southwark
The last surviving galleried coaching inn in London. Built in the 17th century and with plenty of historic features, its wonky, panelled rooms are a delight, and in the summer you can sit outside and imagine plays being performed in its courtyard as onlookers watched from above.

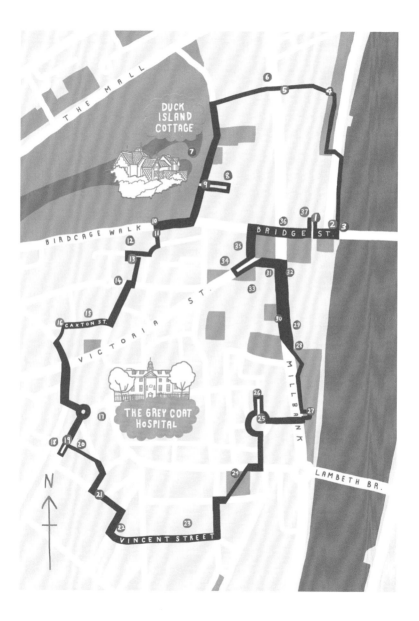

Westminster walk

START

Westminster London
Underground Station

FINISH

Westminster London
Underground Station

DISTANCE

5.4km (3.4 miles)

Westminster is often top of the list of places to see on a first-time visit to London. It contains the iconic clock tower known as Big Ben, the Queen's London residence, Buckingham Palace, and the royal church, Westminster Abbey. It is both the symbolic and the functional heart of the country's power. On this walk you will pass the world-famous building in which many pivotal decisions have been – and continue to be – made.

But away from the tourist hotspots, this can be a surprisingly quiet and residential part of London, with numerous little details and side streets that often get overlooked.

Opposite Palace of Westminster
Right Boudicca's statue

The walk starts at Westminster Station ❶ **Leave via exit 4 and head to Bridge Street, right at the base of Big Ben.** Yes, it is true that Big Ben is actually the nickname of the 13.7-tonne (15.1-ton) bell inside the clock tower, and that the tower's official name is the Elizabeth Tower. As for the name 'Big Ben', although there are various theories, it most likely comes from Sir Benjamin Hall, who oversaw the rebuilding of the Palace of Westminster following a devastating fire in 1834.

The clock tower is just one part of the palace, which was designed by Charles Barry, whose plans were chosen from 97 entries to win the prestigious commission. The majority of the building was complete by 1860. The earlier palace had been built in the 11th century, when this area was known as Thorney Island. You will see some of the surviving buildings from this structure later. Today the palace houses the UK Parliament – made up of the House of Commons and the House of Lords – which makes laws, can set new taxes, holds the government to account and debates issues that affect the whole country.

Cross Victoria Embankment. You will pass a statue of Boudicca, queen of the native British tribe the Iceni ❷ Standing in this location since 1902,

the statue celebrates Boudicca as a fearless leader who led a revolt against the invading Romans around 60 AD, burning London and other cities to the ground in the process. Evidence of this destruction – layers of burnt timber, brick and other objects – are still found during archaeology digs in London today.

Head down the steps beside the sculpture and towards the odd-looking metal object. This is a Thames tide gauge ❸ If you are feeling adventurous, follow the thin metal rungs to climb up part of the structure and peer through the small glass window. It is very dark inside, but you should just about be able to see some red illuminated numbers. They

tell you the current level of the River Thames, measured from mean sea level. The Thames is tidal throughout central London and varies hugely, with a difference in levels of up to 7m (24ft).

Walk north along Westminster Pier and rejoin Victoria Embankment using the steps on your left. A little further on your left is New Scotland Yard, headquarters of the Metropolitan Police since 2016. The name comes from the original location of its headquarters on Whitehall at the time of its foundation in 1829, which had a rear entrance on the street called Great Scotland Yard.

Cross the road to continue through Victoria Embankment Gardens. The gardens contain several war memorials, a fitting location given that the fortress-like stone building on the left is the Ministry of Defence. Walk towards the far side of the building, however, and you will see something far older embedded in grass: a series of stone steps leading to *nowhere* ❹ These are Queen Mary's Steps, a reminder of Whitehall Palace that once stood along the bank of the Thames, roughly between the Palace of Westminster and Trafalgar Square. A jumble of buildings, Whitehall Palace served as the centre of English royal power from 1530 until 1698, and was probably the largest palace in Europe at the time. So, what happened in 1698? Another fire. This time started by a maidservant who was drying linen

sheets too close to a charcoal brazier in a bed chamber.

The steps you see here were built as a convenient river entrance to the palace for Queen Mary II (r. 1689–94) in 1691. You will notice that, today, they seem a rather inconvenient distance from the Thames. This is thanks to the late-19th-century construction of London's sewer system, masterminded by Joseph Bazalgette. Beneath your feet run brick tunnels carrying sewage alongside the Tube tunnels of the District and Circle lines. In total 22 acres of the Thames was embanked, hence these marooned steps.

Turn left along Horse Guards Avenue to reach Whitehall and another reminder of the former

palace. As well as the steps you have just seen, Banqueting House was the only major building to escape the fire and can still be visited today ⑤ It contains the world's only surviving in-situ ceiling paintings by Peter Paul Rubens. Installed in 1639 these staggering works celebrate the reign of the Stuart King James I (r. 1603–25; James VI of Scotland from 1567) and his belief in the divine right of kings.

Above the entrance to Banqueting House you can see a bust of his son Charles I (r. 1625–49); somewhat morbid, as this was the location for his beheading. His execution followed years of fighting between Royalists, loyal to the king, and Oliver Cromwell's Parliamentary Army. The English Civil War (1642–51) was a last resort after the king and Parliament failed to agree on contentious issues that included religion, the king's power and his economic policies. On 30 January 1649, the king was led from Banqueting House onto a scaffold to face a crowd of spectators. His head was severed from his body in one clean stroke and one eyewitness described 'such a groan by the thousands then present as I never heard before and desire I may never hear again'.

Cross Whitehall to stand in front of Horse Guards, a white stone building flanked by two soldiers on

horseback ❻ These are members of the Household Cavalry, regiments of the British Army. Horse Guards was designed by William Kent in the 1740s as the Horse Guards' headquarters. Today it contains some preserved historic rooms as well as the Household Cavalry Museum.

Before you pass through the archway of the building, look up at the golden clock against the white stone cupola of the building and you will notice a dark stain at around 2pm. It is said that this is a permanent mark to remember the execution of King Charles I – a great story, although there is no evidence to back it up! As you walk underneath, look up at the underside of the vaulted stone ceiling. You will see two collections of initials, SFM and St MW. These are parish boundary markers: to the left is the parish of Saint Martin-in-the-Fields and to the right, of Saint Margaret Westminster. Parishes were part of the way London was organized administratively before the introduction of the London Government Act in 1899.

Pass into Horse Guards Parade. Formerly a tiltyard during the reign of King Henry VIII (r. 1509–47) hosting tournaments of sword fighting and jousts, today this is the location of the Queen's official birthday celebration,

On 30 January 1649, the king was led from Banqueting House onto a scaffold to face a crowd of spectators. His head was severed from his body in one clean stroke from a masked executioner

Trooping the Colour. Ahead of you is St James's Park which, in the 13th century, was the site of a leper hospital. King Henry VIII was the first royal to bring it under the Crown's control, acquiring the site in 1532 for hunting. It was only in 1837, with a redesign by John Nash, that it began to look more as it does today, with a lake and romantic vistas.

Skirt the edges of the park, heading south. Shortly on your left you will see some heavily guarded black gates. This is one end of Downing Street, home and office of the prime minister. **Continue south on Horse Guards Road.** Just inside the park on your right you will see the fairytale-like Duck Island Cottage ❼

It was erected by the Ornithological Society of London in 1837, intended for a birdkeeper who was charged with managing the fowl of the park. No one lives there today but the idyllic little building and grounds are now managed by the Royal Parks.

Shortly, on your left as you continue south on Horse Guards Road, you will see Clive Steps, named after Robert Clive who established the military and political supremacy of the East India Company in India and who served two terms as the Governor of Bengal (1758–60 and 1764–67). Returning to Britain between his tenure, he was widely accused of corruption. He later died with a fortune of over £30 million in today's money. At the top of Clive Steps is King Charles Street, flanked by two important government buildings. On the left is the Foreign, Commonwealth & Development Office (finished in 1873 and designed by George Gilbert Scott) and on the right is Her Majesty's Treasury (first designed by William Kent in the 1730s and remodelled by Charles Barry in the 1840s).

On the wall of the Foreign, Commonwealth & Development Office, look out for a plaque dedicated to Ignatius Sancho ❽ Born in Africa c.1729, Sancho was taken to London and worked as a slave for a family in Greenwich. After running away from the family, he was taken in by the 2nd Duke of Montagu who fostered Sancho's talent for reading and writing while he served as a butler and then valet until 1773. Along with his wife Anne, Sancho ran a grocery store near this plaque. As a financially independent homeowner, he was eligible to vote in the 1774 general election, making him the first known person of African descent to vote in a British election.

Head back down the steps towards St James's Park, passing the entrance to Churchill War Rooms on your left ❾ During the Second World War this was a secret headquarters used by the highest government

Right (top) Ignatius Sancho plaque;
(bottom) Queen Anne's Gate

officials, including Prime Minister
Winston Churchill. Hundreds of men
and women worked round the clock
in the underground rooms, and today
the museum – part of the Imperial War
Museum – tells their story.

**Continue to skirt the edge of the
park or enter the park and cut the
corner to exit on Birdcage Walk** ⑩
The name is a reference to the Royal
Aviary established here in the 1600s.
Take in the view across the lake
towards Buckingham Palace, official
London residence of the monarch.
Another curious feature of St James's
Park are the pelicans. The ones you
might see today are part of a tradition
dating back to 1664 when the Russian
Ambassador gave King Charles II
(r. 1660–85) a pair as a gift.

**Once on Birdcage Walk, cross to
Cockpit Steps** ⑪ On a less animal-
friendly note, this is a reference to the
Royal Cockpit, a venue for cockfighting
that stood close to here until it was
demolished in 1810. **Turn right at
the top of the steps to enter Queen
Anne's Gate** ⑫ This street contains a
number of listed properties from the
18th century and no. 1 on your left –
previously three townhouses – has
recently been refurbished into private
flats. The five-bedroom penthouse
was available for £22 million in 2020.
You would be in good company living

Left (top) Victor Tyre Company mosaic; **(bottom)** 55 Broadway

at this address, as the street has one of the highest concentrations of blue plaques anywhere in London, mainly remembering politicians and statesmen who worked nearby.

Head south on Carteret Street, looking out for a lovely mosaic on the right ⑬ This is a surviving remnant of a 'ghost' advertisement from the early 1900s for Victor Tyre Company who had their head office nearby. As you reach Tothill Street, look left for a fantastic view of Westminster Abbey. You will get a closer look later on, but for now cross into Broadway. The weighty stone building on the corner is 55 Broadway ⑭ It served as the purpose-built headquarters of Transport for London from 1929 until the company moved out in 2020. The plans are to convert it into a hotel.

Follow the map to turn right onto Caxton Street, to reach the former Caxton Hall ⑮ The name is a reference to William Caxton, who in 1476 established the first English printing press in Westminster. The hall was completed in 1882 and used as a town hall for events and weddings, but was also a key campaign site for the Women's Social and Political Union (WSPU), which fought for women's suffrage. In 1906 Caxton Hall was chosen as the venue for the group's first large meeting in

Charity schools were one of the few ways in which poorer children were able to receive teaching before the Education Act of 1870.

London and more than 400 women attended. Following the meeting they marched to the House of Commons in Parliament to lobby MPs, and one year later they held the first 'Women's Parliament' in this same venue. The hall closed in 1977 and was redeveloped into flats and offices in 2006.

Continue along Caxton Street until you see a cute redbrick building on your left. In the niche above the doorway stands a statue of a young boy in a blue coat ❶❻ He stands as a reminder that this was once a Blue Coat charity school, built in 1709. Charity schools were one of the few ways in which poorer children were able to receive teaching before the Education Act of 1870. They were often named after their distinctive uniform colours, provided for free.

Follow the map through Brewer's Green to reach Buckingham Gate and on to Victoria Street; cross the

Opposite (top) Caxton Hall; **(bottom)**
Former Blue Coat charity school
Right The Albert pub

road here. Intended as a new modern artery for London, Victoria Street was laid out in the mid-1800s, clearing away haphazard collections of slum housing. After crossing, look back to admire The Albert pub, built in the 1860s and one of the few surviving Victorian buildings on the otherwise redeveloped street. **From here, head south on Artillery Row.** Don't miss the view to your right along Howick Place, offering a glimpse of the impressive red-and-white tower of Westminster Cathedral. Its foundation stone was laid in 1895, but the interior of the cathedral, although impressive, remains unfinished, with works taking place when funding allows.

Ahead is The Greencoat Boy pub, which, like the former Blue Coat statue you saw earlier, is a reference to a charitable institution in the area. A third, which can also be seen ahead, is Grey Coat Hospital **17** Founded in 1698 as a charitable boarding school, today this is still a working secondary school and the central block dates from 1701. The reason behind all these charitable concerns was that during the 19th century this area was known as the 'Devil's Acre', one of the worst slums in London. The name was coined by Charles Dickens writing in his magazine *Household Words* in 1850 and refers to the overcrowded housing

that was prone to flooding and in a semi-derelict condition. By the late 19th century Victoria Street had ploughed through the worst aspects and new blocks of industrial dwellings – good-quality housing for the poor – were being introduced in an attempt to improve the situation.

Continue south on Rochester Row. You will see the redbrick Westminster Almshouse on your right, charity housing built in the 1880s, which replaced earlier 18th-century almshouses on the same site **18**

Retrace your steps to head right on Rochester Street, passing the impressive St Stephen's Church **19** The foundation stone was laid in 1847 and it was designed by Benjamin

Left (top) Westminster Almshouse; **(centre)** Ancient Lights, Rochester Street; **(bottom)** Vincent Street fireplace

Ferrey, a pupil of Augustus Pugin who worked alongside Charles Barry on the Houses of Parliament.

While on Rochester Street, look up to see two boards declaring 'Ancient Lights' on the side of the primary school ⑳ These are reminders of a historic common law giving private property owners the right to daylight. The school itself was funded by Angela Burdett-Coutts, an heiress and one of the most generous philanthropists in the Victorian era. She also paid for the building of St Stephen's Church as a memorial to her parents who both died in 1844. Her aim was to bring education and Christianity into the slums of South Westminster.

Turn right into Greycoat Lane and Elverton Street then turn left into Vincent Square ㉑ The 13-acre site is named after William Vincent, a former dean of Westminster Abbey and headmaster of Westminster School who, in the early 1800s, wanted to ensure the grounds weren't developed and lost to further housing projects. He hired a ploughman to dig a ditch around the perimeter of the square, ensuring that it be kept as open playing grounds for the school, which it remains to this day.

Walk around the square until you turn into Vincent Street. Shortly, on your left, tucked in among the ivy

after the Thames flooded in 1928. **On reaching the end of Vincent Street, head left into Marsham Street and then right into Page Street to cross through St John's Gardens ㉔** This is the former burial ground of the church of St John's, Smith Square, which you will also see shortly. The land was consecrated in 1731 but within only 50 years it required a high wall and two watchmen to deter body snatchers intent on stealing fresh corpses for medical study. As with many parish graveyards in 19th-century London, the burial ground was becoming unbearably overcrowded and a gruesome public nuisance. It was closed in 1853 and transformed into a public garden, opening in 1885.

Exit the gardens onto Horseferry Road. It is named after a ferry between here and Lambeth that would carry horses, carriages and passengers on a long platform across the river. The earliest mention of a horse ferry here is 1513. **Continue north on Dean Bradley Street to enter Smith Square ㉕** Here stands the former church of St John the Evangelist. Designed by Thomas Archer, the church was built between 1714 and 1728 and is one of the most elaborate (and expensive) of the Commission for Building Fifty New Churches Act. It cost the equivalent of £5.2 million

beside a black gate that closes off a residential development, is one of the most curious survivors in London – an internal fireplace that once belonged to a terrace of houses destroyed in the Blitz ㉒ Today new housing has been built around it, but it is a haunting reminder of domestic cosiness disrupted by bombs. Without so much as a plaque explaining its history, it just waits patiently and poignantly until someone stumbles across it.

Continue along Vincent Street, passing a redbrick housing estate on your left before reaching the dazzling chequerboard flats of the Grosvenor Estate ㉓ Designed by Edwin Lutyens in 1929–35, these buildings replaced a group of dilapidated houses damaged

Right (top) Smith Square; **(bottom)** Lord North Street bomb shelters

today. It now serves as a popular concert venue.

Walk around the church towards the left-hand side and take a brief detour up Lord North Street. On the left is a plaque to William Thomas Stead, who became the youngest editor in the country at the age of 22, of the *Pall Mall Gazette* in 1871. The newspaper (absorbed into the *Evening Standard* in 1923) was highly influential and under Stead's control was responsible for pushing an agenda of liberal reforms in terms of child welfare, the age of consent and laws intended to deter sex work. He died on board the RMS *Titanic* in 1912, reportedly giving his life jacket to another passenger.

Further up Lord North Street, look a bit closer at the houses to see some intriguing historic reminders. The basements were used as shelters during the Blitz, indicated by the faded arrows, 'S's (denoting 'shelter') and written instructions **26** **Retrace your steps and exit Smith Square to head east on Dean Stanley Street from where you can enter Victoria Tower Gardens.** Ahead of you is the glorious Buxton Memorial, a multicoloured former water fountain whose pretty, jewel-like appearance hides a darker bit of British history **27** This is a memorial dedicated to Sir Thomas Fowell Buxton, an MP who campaigned to end slavery in the early 1800s. Although the transatlantic slave trade had been abolished in 1807, slavery still took place within the British Empire. In 1823 Buxton cofounded the Anti-Slavery Society alongside William Wilberforce; it was only after several failed attempts to introduce the law

Right (top) Buxton Memorial; **(bottom)** Victoria Tower

that, in 1833, the Slavery Abolition Act was finally passed, making the purchase or ownership of slaves illegal in most parts of the empire.

Follow the map north, through Victoria Tower Gardens. At the far end of the park stands a statue of Emmeline Pankhurst, founder of the WSPU that you encountered at Caxton Hall, and a leading figure in the fight for votes for women ❷❽ As you exit the gardens onto Abingdon Street, you will pass Victoria Tower on your right ❷❾ Today, the tower houses the Parliamentary Archives, around 9.6km (6 miles) worth of shelving containing documents, records and laws. Tours of the archive are occasionally run, and it is well worth looking out for these for a chance to enter the Act Room: 64,000 vellum rolls of Acts of Parliament that date back to 1497. As well as the archives, the tower serves as the Sovereign's Entrance, used by the monarch when they arrive for the State Opening of Parliament.

Opposite Victoria Tower stands an older stone building: Jewel Tower ❸⓿ Built in the 1360s it was intended as a storeroom for royal treasure as part of the medieval Palace of Westminster. Today it is run by English Heritage and contains a small museum.

Continue on Abingdon Street, with the Houses of Parliament on your

right. You are looking at a 16th-century extension of Westminster Abbey known as the Henry VII Chapel. Within the stonework is a small hole made by a bomb that exploded in this street on 27 September 1940.

Further ahead on the left is St Margaret's Church, the parish church of the House of Commons ❸ First built in the 12th century, this served the local population rather than the Benedictine monks who were based in Westminster Abbey. Unsurprisingly it has strong connections with Parliament today and is where Prime Minister Winston Churchill married Clementine Hozier in 1908. An easily missed detail can be seen on the side of St Margaret's Church: a bust of King Charles I, ironically looking over towards Parliament and the statue of Oliver Cromwell, his successor ❷

Turn left to walk along Broad Sanctuary to appreciate the scale and drama of Westminster Abbey ❸ A royal church, this is the final resting place of more than 30 kings and queens as well as eminent Britons that include Charles Darwin, Isaac Newton and Stephen Hawking.

Established in 960 AD, when this area was merely a patch of flooded marshland known as Thorney Island, the bulk of the building you see today dates from a 13th-century

rebuild under King Henry III (r. 1216–72). Immediately on passing St Margaret's Church, you will see the abbey's north entrance, with its flying buttresses and majestic rose window. At the western end, the two towers were added by Nicholas Hawksmoor in the 1740s. Today they mark the grand entrance used for coronations and royal weddings. But not all of this frontage is centuries old. The row of 10 statues above the door is known collectively as the Modern Martyrs. Unveiled in 1998, the statues commemorate 20th-century Christians from around the world who have been oppressed or persecuted for their faith; fifth from the left is Martin Luther King Jr, Baptist minister, activist and leader of the American Civil Rights Movement, who was assassinated in 1968.

Cross Broad Sanctuary to retrace your steps, but on the opposite side of the street, and take a left down Little Sanctuary. You are now standing behind the Supreme Court, the highest court in the country and final court of appeal. Somewhat ironically situated here, is a doorway to nowhere that serves as a reminder to a far less democratic institution ❸ For this door was once part of the Westminster Bridewell, a prison that stood here from the

Right (top) Jewel Tower; (bottom) Supreme Court

17th century until the institute was demolished in 1834.

Return to Broad Sanctuary and follow it around Parliament Square. Look up to admire the frieze on the front of the Supreme Court, completed in the early 1900s ❸❺ This famous square houses statues of former British prime ministers and international politicians. Since 2018, a woman has been honoured among the statues – Millicent Garrett Fawcett, who campaigned for votes for women.

On the northern edge of the square, look up at the building on the corner of Great George Street and Parliament Street to see a green plaque in memory of John Peake Knight, an engineer who created the world's first traffic light, installed here in 1868 ❸❻ Based on railway signalling systems, it would have directed horses and carts, but sadly was a little ahead of its time. Powered by gas, after just one month, the structure exploded; traffic lights wouldn't be common across London for another 40 years. You are now a few minutes from the entrance to Westminster Station, where the walk ends ❸❼

IN FOCUS • BLUE PLAQUES

If you need a starting point for looking up in London, blue plaques are a good place to begin.

LET'S TAKE A CLOSER LOOK

London boasts the oldest blue plaque scheme in the United Kingdom, begun by the Royal Society of Arts in 1866. The aim was to celebrate and commemorate famous figures through the places in which they lived, worked and died.

In 1867 the first official blue plaque was awarded to Lord Byron, however the building was demolished in 1889, the plaque disappearing with it. The oldest blue plaque around today is on King Street, SW1 (see page 71). In 1901 the London County Council (LCC) took over the scheme and, from 1965, the Greater London Council (GLC) expanded it beyond Central London.

Today, having a blue plaque on a building can sometimes be the lynchpin for its survival. By helping to raise awareness about the historic importance of a building, it can ensure its preservation. This was the case at 48 Doughty Street, now the Charles Dickens Museum (see page 77), where the plaque was erected in 1903, well before it became a museum in 1925. While it does not offer watertight legal protection, having a blue plaque can also help to get a building listed (and therefore protected)

Opposite (top) Oldest surviving plaque; **(centre)** LCC plaque; **(bottom)** Dr Johnson's brown plaque
Above John Snow's plaque

by Historic England. This was the case with D.H. Lawrence's blue plaque in Hampstead.

Out of the blue

Confusingly, not all plaques are blue, or even round! The City of London has its own scheme of square plaques aside from a unique round brown plaque dedicated to Dr Samuel Johnson, who wrote the *English Dictionary*. His plaque is at 17 Gough Square, his former house, and now a wonderful museum. There's also an octagonal plaque that remembers Dr John Snow, father of epidemiology, in Soho.

Other London boroughs and societies have developed their own, independent, plaque schemes, so you can expect to find green, red, brown and blue all over. In fact, anyone can set up their own blue plaque scheme and there are plenty of rogue ones to be found!

The English Heritage scheme

In terms of recognizing the official blue plaques, you can look out for a few key details. Since 1984 all English Heritage plaques are painstakingly handmade by Frank and Sue Ashworth. The slightly domed ceramic roundels are fired in a kiln and glazed in blue. This shape encourages self-cleaning with rainwater. Then raised, hand-piped, white lettering is applied with the English Heritage name around the top and its logo at the bottom.

There are exceptions, of course. A favourite geeky detail is that four plaques commemorating the founding fathers of the London Underground all have the world-famous Johnston typeface, used throughout the network.

There are also, on occasions, mistakes. London's habit of repeatedly renumbering streets means sometimes plaques are put up at the wrong addresses, but there are also other fun errors you can spot. Thomas Arne has been curiously cropped and Thomas De Quincey has had his name spelt wrong! Both can be found in Covent Garden.

In general the organization tries to limit plaques to one per person*, and at least one building that they're associated with must survive within Greater London. This building cannot be any old venue that many people have visited (such as a church or a pub) and has to

be visible from a public highway and not have been substantially altered beyond the recognition of the nominee. Finally, no more than two plaques are allowed on any one building.

With a scheme that has been running for more than 150 years, of course, things have changed over time. As of 2016 women only accounted for 13 per cent of blue plaques, with black and ethnic minority figures accounting for less than 5 per cent. So, if you know a historic, unsung hero or heroine who deserves a blue plaque, you can nominate them on the English Heritage website. (www.english-heritage.org.uk/visit/blue-plaques/propose-a-plaque/)

* Counting all types of plaque across the United Kingdom, John Wesley has the most (a whopping 47!). But Charles Dickens is right behind him with 43.

Opposite (top) Green plaque in memory of Edith Garrud; **(centre)** English Heritage plaque; **(bottom)** plaque with Johnston typeface
Above (top) Thomas Arne plaque; **(bottom)** John Wesley plaque

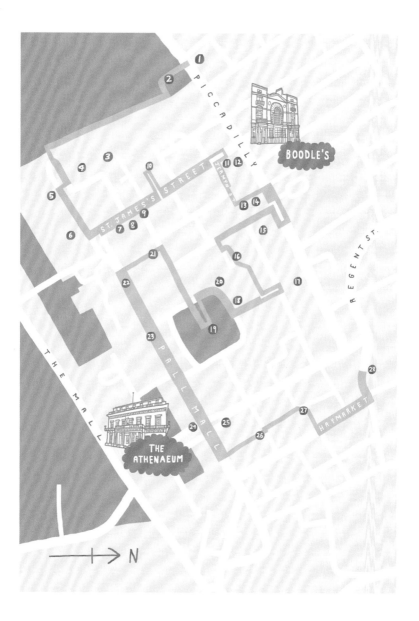

St James's walk

START
Green Park London
Underground Station

FINISH
Piccadilly London
Underground Station

DISTANCE
3km (1.9 miles)

St James's is a small, elegant neighbourhood within the borough of Westminster. It lies between Piccadilly to the north and The Mall and St James's Park to the south. Green Park skirts its westernmost edges, while Haymarket marks its eastern boundary.

A number of impressive historic houses and luxury businesses stand testimony to this area becoming a royal enclave and home to aristocrats in the 17th century, spurring an influx of shopkeepers, outfitters and suppliers. Today, St James's is known for a number of London's most prestigious private members' clubs and high-end shops.

Right (top) Diana Fountain;
(bottom) St James's Park gas lamp
Opposite Spencer House

The walk starts at Green Park Station
❶ **If you are arriving by Tube, follow
the exit towards Green Park and
Buckingham Palace.** A ramp will take
you to the corner of the park and
the black and gold sculptural Diana
Fountain ❷ You are now standing on
the edge of Green Park, a 42-acre open
space that used to house the St James's
leper hospital, founded before 1100.
The sculptural fountain depicts Diana,
Roman goddess of the hunt, and is an
apt reminder that this area started to
take shape under King Henry VIII
(r. 1509–47), who secured the land for
use as private hunting grounds in the
1500s. You will see the palace he built
in the area shortly.

Follow the map to walk along the
path at the far edge of the park. Look
out for the historic gas lamps dating
back to the early 1800s that line the
route. These are some of the 1,500
surviving gas lamps that are looked
after by British Gas today (read more
on pages 210–211). Green Park has
only been open to the public since
1826. King Charles II (r. 1660–85)
had enclosed the grounds as a deer
park in 1668, after which it served
as an exclusive venue for royals and
aristocrats to socialize, relax and scout
for prospective spouses. Along the
left-hand side of the park are a few
mansions that remind us of this lost

world; among the finest of the 18th-century survivors is Spencer House ❸

It is not easy to get a good view of Spencer House from the park, but you can admire the stone facade and rooftop sculptures through the trees. It was constructed in 1756-8 under the designs of John Vardy (and subsequently James 'Athenian' Stuart) for the 1st Earl Spencer and his wife Georgiana. Their daughter, also Georgiana, is probably the most famous character associated with the building. A charismatic and beautiful author, style icon and activist, she married the 5th Duke of Devonshire, one of the most eligible bachelors of the age. The marriage was not a happy one, with the Duke pursuing various

affairs while Georgiana struggled to produce a much-sought-after male heir. Their strained relationship reached a peak of unconventionality when Georgiana's best friend 'Bess' moved into the household, establishing a ménage à trois. Georgiana did, eventually, produce an heir, but her eventful life was marked with tragedy. The Earl Spencer banished her from England between 1791 and 1793 while she gave birth to a daughter by her lover, Earl Grey; then, as she grew older, she was consumed by addictions to laudanum and gambling, dying at the young age of 48. The 2008 film *The Duchess* is based on her life, and Georgiana is the great-great-great-great aunt of Diana, Princess of Wales.

Today Spencer House is owned by the Rothschild Foundation and is available to visit on pre-booked tours.

Follow the map left down a narrow alley to join Cleveland Row alongside Bridgewater House ④ Designed as a residential home in the mid-19th century by Charles Barry, it was converted into private offices after bomb damage sustained in the Second World War. The building was bought by a Greek shipping magnate in 1981 and continues to be held in their family. **Continue along Cleveland Row until you see the redbrick walls of St James's Palace.** In the gap on the right-hand side, guarded by armed policemen, is the sandy-coloured Lancaster House ⑤ Once an aristocratic home, today it is owned by the government and used for hospitality events and conferences. The impressive building is also regularly used for filming, often featuring as a stand-in for Buckingham Palace, and appears in *The King's Speech* as well as Netflix's *The Crown*.

Still on Cleveland Row, walk along the side of St James's Palace until you see the gatehouse ⑥ This is the earliest surviving part of the palace, which was built in the 1530s for King Henry VIII and is still the most senior royal palace today – it even ranks above Buckingham Palace, which

usurped it as the official London residence of the monarch under Queen Victoria (r. 1837–1901) in 1837. Ambassadors are still appointed to the Court of St James's, and it is in St James's Palace that the Accession Council meets following the death of a monarch and from where they announce the new sovereign.

Turn left onto St James's Street and cross the road. Ahead is the grand facade of wine merchants Berry Bros. & Rudd ⑦ The shopfront dates from the 19th century, but the rest of the building is far older, constructed in the 1730s. The history of the shop goes back farther still; a coffeehouse was established here in 1698 by a woman known as the Widow Bourne, and if you look up at the hanging shop sign, you will see the symbol of the coffee mill remembering this history.

If Berry Bros. & Rudd is open, it is well worth going inside the shop to see its collection of memorabilia, including huge 18th-century weighing scales and a framed telegram from the ill-fated RMS *Titanic*, confirming the loss of a shipment of wine on board. An archway in the shop's facade leads to Pickering Place, a 17th-century alleyway, flanked on the right by an 18th-century timber-framed wall. It is named after the Widow Bourne's son-in-law, William Pickering, who

Left (top) St James's gatehouse;
(bottom) Berry Bros. & Rudd

took over the running of the shop in the 1700s. **Take a short detour down this narrow alley.** Immediately on the right, you will see a brass plaque declaring that, between 1842 and 1845, this was the site of the Texas Legation, a kind of embassy before the state officially joined the United States of America on 29 December 1845. **Continue along the alleyway, and you will enter one of London's smallest public squares.** From here you can admire the offices and event spaces of Berry Bros. & Rudd. Sadly, Westminster City Council have replaced the two historic gas lamps with LED replicas.

Return along Pickering Place to St James's Street; turn right to admire two more historic shops. At no. 6 St James's Street is Lock & Co. Hatters, established in 1676 and located here since 1765 ❽ As well as selling hats for men and women, the shop houses a small museum of famous headgear, including Admiral Nelson's bicorne, the top hat worn by Winston Churchill on his wedding day, and a conformateur – an elaborate measuring device to ensure a perfect-fitting hat.

A few doors up at no. 9 is Lobb, a bespoke shoemaker established in the 19th century ❾ Above the shop entrance you will see two coats of arms, a familiar site in this area. These are royal warrants, marks that confirm

Right Boodle's
Opposite White's

at least five years of supplying goods or services to the royal household. They can be granted by Queen Elizabeth or the Prince of Wales, and formerly the Duke of Edinburgh. Very occasionally an establishment may receive warrants from all three!

Cross the street and follow the map to enter the easily missed Blue Ball Yard ❿ Originally 18th-century stables, today this courtyard contains the outside seating of the Stafford Hotel's American Bar.

Return to St James's Street and continue towards the top end of the street to admire two of the oldest clubs in the area. The first is at no. 28, with a spectacular arched central window and built in 1775–6 ⓫ This is Boodle's, one of many private gentlemen's clubs in the area that sprung up in the 18th century as centres for networking, socializing and gambling. For aristocratic young men who had a country seat but felt a little overwhelmed by London, these establishments provided a home-from-home, sometimes even offering rooms for overnight stays. Boodle's takes its name from its first head waiter to serve here and was founded in 1762. Originally based at 49–51 Pall Mall, it moved to this location in 1782.

Boodle's is often seen as a rival to White's Club at no. 37 ⓬ White's was founded in 1693, making it the oldest gentlemen's club in London. It takes its name from Francesco Bianco, an Italian immigrant who ran a hot chocolate shop on Curzon Street, Mayfair, and acted as a kind of concierge and fixer, supplying the well-to-do with theatre tickets. The club formed around like-minded gentlemen from the Curzon Street HQ before they moved here in the 1770s. It is now known as one of the most exclusive clubs in the world, counting Prince Charles and former prime ministers amongst its members.

Having admired White's, retrace your steps to enter Jermyn Street on the left. The name comes from Henry Jermyn, Earl of St Albans, who developed the surrounding streets

as a residential and commercial suburb of the Court of St James's in the 17th century. Ahead you will see the statue of an exemplary St James's gentleman, George 'Beau' Brummell, a fashionable dandy and socialite who typified Regency England 🔞 Brummell began his career in the military, part of a cavalry regiment under the Prince of Wales (later King George IV, r. 1820–30), and the two became friends. When the regiment was to be stationed in Manchester in the 1790s, Brummell left the army to launch himself into London society. He used his friendship with the king to cultivate lavish habits and adopted a distinct style of dress. Breaking from the style of the time, he rejected the customary gaudy and patterned men's clothes, instead opting for minimalist block colours, long dark coats and crisp white cravats. At over 1.8m (6ft) tall, and slim, he cut a fine figure through St James's and Mayfair, but his dry sense of humour, overspending and gambling habits resulted in a rather spectacular fall from grace.

Brummell's biographer William Jesse, writing in 1844, shares an anecdote of the Prince Regent and Beau falling out at a party when the prince ignored Brummell in front of fellow guests. Brummell's response was to loudly enquire 'Who's your fat friend?', gesturing at the overweight prince. No doubt satisfying in the short term, this was a step too far for

Beau. Without royal protection, Beau's creditors started demanding payment for their hefty outstanding bills, not to mention the tabs he had run up at White's and Boodle's. In a bid to escape debtors' prison, Brummell fled to France in 1816 and lived out the rest of his days in exile. **Follow Brummell's gaze and walk up the charming Piccadilly Arcade**, designed by George Thrale Jell in 1908 **14**

At the end of Piccadilly Arcade, you arrive onto Piccadilly, the boundary between St James's and Mayfair. Today, one of the busiest streets in the West End, it was once a 16th-century lane through fields. The name is derived from the 'pickadill', a stiff collar invented by the tailor Robert Baker who had a house built near today's Piccadilly Circus in 1612. The house gained the nickname Piccadilly Hall and the name stuck.

Another, earlier, historic reminder survives in the form of Burlington House opposite. Today the building houses various clubs and society offices, most notably the Royal Academy of Arts. However, it was once a 17th-century mansion house surrounded by greenery. The building we see today dates from a renovation for Lord George Cavendish by Samuel Ware in 1815–18. The Cavendish coat of arms can be seen above Burlington

Arcade, laid out in 1819, which you may want to take a short detour through.

Otherwise follow the map right, a short distance along Piccadilly, to reach Fortnum & Mason 15 Although the actual fabric of the building is 20th century, the shop itself was established in 1707 by William Fortnum and Hugh Mason. The two were footmen working in the household of Queen Anne (r. 1702–07), who set up a high-end grocer's selling provisions to local wealthy clients. Among the shop's more surprising claims to fame are the facts that, in 1738, it invented the Scotch egg and, in 1886, it was the first English shop to sell Heinz Baked Beans. Carefully cross over to the traffic island in the centre of Piccadilly to look up and better admire the 1964 rococo-style clock. On the hour, Mr Fortnum and Mr Mason appear from their huts and bow to one another.

Cross back to Fortnum & Mason and follow the map down Duke Street St James's towards Chequers Tavern, set within an 18th-century building. The ground floor looks late 19th century, but there has been a pub here – previously known as the Mason's Arms – since the early 1700s. **Follow the map down the side alley to enter the surprisingly large Mason's Yard.** Laid out by 1682 and used to stable horse and carriages, rather than

Left (top) Fortnum & Mason;
(bottom) St James's, Piccadilly

a connection with stone masonry, the name probably comes from early 18th-century landowners Henry and William Mason who owned some of the surrounding houses.

The great hulking block in the centre of Mason's Yard is a reminder that, from the 20th century, the square housed an electricity substation, demolished and replaced by White Cube art gallery which opened in 2006 ⑯ While the walk so far has featured mainly aristocrats and royals, Mason's Yard provides a refreshing burst of more contemporary music history. It was at Indica Gallery (no. 6) that, in 1966, John Lennon met Yoko Ono, who was hosting a show of her artwork. At The Scotch of St James (no. 13) that same year, Jimi Hendrix played his first London gig and met his girlfriend, Kathy Etchingham.

Exit Mason's Yard via Ormond Yard and into Duke of York Street. Turn left towards Piccadilly. You will have a nice view of St James's, Piccadilly ⑰ Built 1676–84, this is one of the few churches by Christopher Wren outside of the City of London. **Retrace your steps to walk down Duke of York Street towards St James's Square, the focal point of Henry Jermyn's property development.** On the wall of 10 Duke of York Street is a plaque to Jermyn, as

Left (top) 10 Duke of York Street;
(bottom) the London Library

well as a pair of curious cone-shaped structures either side of the front door ⑱ These are surviving 'snuffers', a reminder of a time before electric streetlighting when servants would snuff out the flaming torches that had lit the way home for their masters.

If the gates are open you may want to step inside St James's Square, bought by Jermyn in 1661, which makes it – aside from Covent Garden – the first of London's true West End squares ⑲ Conveniently situated close to St James's Palace, its aim was to provide 'great and good houses' for courtiers. Jermyn's plan worked; by 1721 six dukes and seven earls had houses here, and today there are many blue plaques celebrating famous and notable residents.

On the northwest side of the square, at no. 10, stands Chatham House, an international affairs think-tank founded in 1920 and the originator of the Chatham House Rule by which any information discussed can be shared, but the source of the information cannot be revealed. The house was built in the 1730s, and as you can see on the blue plaque, it has been a popular address for politicians, with three prime ministers having lived here throughout its history.

At no. 12 is another blue plaque, but this time for a woman: Ada Lovelace.

Left Sculptural reliefs in Angel Court

A mathematician and writer, Lovelace worked with Charles Babbage on his computer while living here in the 1830s. She published the first computer algorithm, realizing that the machine's potential extended far beyond calculations.

Tucked in the top northwest corner of St James's Square is the London Library, one of the most remarkable spaces in the city ❷⓿ You wouldn't guess from the outside, but this is the largest independent lending library in the world, hiding 27km (17 miles) of shelving behind its front doors. The library was founded in 1841 by Thomas Carlyle (see page 204) in response to his frustration at the strictness of the British Library and need for a new

lending library. Though it is only for members, it is straightforward to join and you can also visit on a public tour.

Follow the map out of St James's Square and onto King Street. Outside no. 3, look up to see the oldest surviving blue plaque in London, erected in 1867 to commemorate the fact that Napoleon III (first president of France and nephew of the more famous Napoleon I) lived here in 1848. At no. 8 King Street is Christie's, the world's oldest fine art auctioneer. The auction house's first sale was conducted by James Christie in 1766 near Oxford Street and it moved to this location in 1823.

On reaching the attractive Victorian pub, The Golden Lion, follow the map to turn left into Angel Court ❷❶ This was once the site of St James's Theatre, established in 1835. It was largely unsuccessful until the late 1800s when it hosted plays by Oscar Wilde, including *Lady Windermere's Fan* and *The Importance of Being Earnest*. In 1950 Laurence Olivier and his wife Vivien Leigh managed the theatre, and this history is commemorated in a sculptural relief on the wall of Angel Court with the couple reprising their most famous roles as Antony and Cleopatra. Despite protests, the theatre was demolished in 1957. Further along Angel Court are

Opposite (left) 89 Pall Mall;
(right) The Reform Club

sculptural reliefs by Edward Bainbridge Copnall that were originally on the front of the theatre. They depict George Alexander, manager of the theatre 1890–1918, Oscar Wilde and Gilbert Miller, the final owner. Each are flanked by scenes of productions under their tenure (or in Wilde's case, those he wrote).

Exit Angel Court onto Pall Mall. Pall Mall was laid out in 1661 and takes its name from the ball game *paille-maille* (in French) or *palla maglio* (in Italian). Today it is most famous for its numerous gentlemen's clubs and most of the south side of the street is owned by the Crown Estate. There is one curious exception however at no. 79 where – if you look up – you can see a blue plaque to Nell Gwyn, mistress of Charles II **22** A beautiful and talented actress, Nell caught the king's attention when performing at the Theatre Royal Drury Lane, and her plucky intelligence and charm ensured she carved out a comfortable life for herself. No. 79 Pall Mall stands on the site of the brick townhouse that she occupied on retiring from acting and, in 1676, she seems to have persuaded Charles II to grant the freehold of the building to trustees of the Earl of St Alban's estate. They, in turn, conveyed it to her for life. It was the property of her sons until 1693 and today remains

The Reform Club was among the first along Pall Mall to admit women, its first female member joining in 1981.

the only freehold on this side of the street not owned by the Crown.

Next door (no. 80–2) is Schomberg House, one of very few surviving grand 17th-century homes in London, built for the Duke of Schomberg in 1698. The decorative cream porch, with muscular men holding up a reclining female, dates from 1791, when the building was used by the Polygraphic Society that hosted annual exhibitions of reproductions of paintings. With its blue flag hanging over into the street, the Royal Automobile Club at no. 89 Pall Mall is probably the most impressive of the clubs of St James's **23** It is certainly the largest, built as a steel-framed construction and designed by Mewes and Davies in

1908–11. The club began in 1895, with the creation of the Self-Propelled Traffic Association, which aimed to encourage the use of automobiles or 'horseless carriages' nationally.

On the facade of no. 108, look out for a plaque commemorating Frederick Winsor and the fact that Pall Mall was the world's first street to be lit by gas lamps. Further along, at no. 104, is the dark green door of the Reform Club, founded in 1836, and – as the name suggests – a meeting place for those passionate about the passing of the Great Reform Act of 1832, a law that hugely increased the number of eligible (male) voters across the country. Completed in 1841, the building was designed by Charles Barry

(who you saw earlier at Bridgewater House and is most famous for the Houses of Parliament). This club was among the first along Pall Mall to admit women, its first female member joining in 1981. Next door is The Travellers Club, also designed by Charles Barry between 1829 and 1832. This club was established in 1819, making it the oldest on Pall Mall, and its original concept was to restrict membership to those who had travelled at least 800km (500 miles) from London in a direct line. In today's age of long-haul flights this seems a small distance, but at the time, in the wake of the Napoleonic Wars across Europe, it was envisaged as a place to welcome the most exclusive foreign visitors and diplomats.

Right The Athenaeum
Opposite Florence Nightingale statue

Our final club, on the corner of Pall Mall and Waterloo Place, is The Athenaeum, established in 1824 as a club for artists and literary men who were defined by their intelligence and achievements rather than background or politics ㉔ Of all the clubs it can boast the most Nobel Prize winners – more than 50 with representation in every category. The clubhouse was designed by Decimus Burton and built between 1827 and 1830. The name is from the ancient Roman Athenaeum, for literary and scientific studies. In keeping with this theme, the facade of the house boasts a huge golden statue of the Greek goddess of wisdom, Athena, and along the top in white and blue is a copy of the Parthenon frieze. The Athenaeum admitted its first female member in 2002.

Cross Pall Mall at Waterloo Place. Stop to admire the huge Guards Crimean War Memorial, installed in 1861. The figure of Sidney Herbert, secretary of state at war during the conflict, was unveiled in 1867. Also here, the statue of Florence Nightingale, 'Lady of the Lamp' and mother of modern nursing who helped soldiers during the same war, was not added until 1915 ㉕ **From here, cut through the Royal Opera Arcade, on your left a little further along Pall Mall** ㉖ It may not be as dazzling as

The Athenaeum, established in 1824 as a club for artists and literary men who were defined by their intelligence and achievements rather than background or politics. Of all the clubs it can boast the most Nobel Prize winners – more than 50 with representation in every category.

the Piccadilly Arcade you saw earlier, but this is London's first shopping arcade, laid out 1816–18 to the designs of John Nash. As you exit the arcade and cross Charles II Street, look right to admire the facade of the Theatre Royal Haymarket, also by John Nash and dating from 1820–1.

Cross Charles II Street to continue your walk along the largely pedestrianized St Alban's Street to reach St James's Market ㉗ This area has been thoroughly renovated but it stands near the site of the original market established in 1663 as part of the development plans by Henry Jermyn. Today it offers a cluster of smart cafes and restaurants, but the earlier rural history is also remembered in the name of nearby Haymarket, first paved in 1692 on the site of the market founded in the 16th century. **Turn right off St Alban's Street at Norris Street to reach Haymarket.** Try to bear its quieter, rural history in mind as you follow this now frenetic street towards Piccadilly Circus Station, where the walk ends ㉘

TOP 10 · UNUSUAL MUSEUMS

London isn't short of world-class museums. Millions of people visit the British Museum, Tate Modern and Britain and the National Gallery each year, but the city also boasts hundreds of small, quirky museums that are well worth exploring.

1. Foundling Museum, WCl

Sits on the site, and tells the story of the Foundling Hospital, established in 1739 as an orphanage for abandoned children. Highlights include preserved historic rooms, moving personal objects and a collection of contemporary art.

2. Dennis Severs House, E1

Arriving in London from America in 1979, Dennis Severs became enthralled by the history of this 18th-century Spitalfields townhouse. Refurbishing its rooms, he created a space that is now part-museum, part-immersive theatre.

3. Sir John Soane's Museum, WC2

Each inch of this house is covered in the ideas and experiments of one of the foremost architects of the 18th century, alongside his collection of Egyptian artefacts and paintings.

4. Old Operating Theatre, SE1

Hidden inside an early-18th-century church by London Bridge is the last surviving 19th-century operating theatre in Europe. The museum tells the history of early medicine and surgery amid the atmospheric surroundings of the church's attic roof.

5. Crossness Pumping Station, SE2

Constructed from beautiful, brightly coloured Victorian ironwork, Crossness contains the world's largest rotative beam engine. It is also a fascinating testament to the ways in which an ever-growing city manages its waste and tackles pollution and water-borne diseases.

6. Bow Street Police Museum, WC2

This museum, set within London's first police station, offers a chance to see inside the former cells and to stand in the old Bow Street Magistrates dock.

7. Leighton House Museum, W14

The former home and studio of celebrated Victorian painter, Lord Frederick Leighton. As well as many of his paintings, it contains some of the most exquisite interiors in London. Among them is the Arab Hall, a tiled space complete with a fountain that Leighton designed after visiting North Africa and the Middle East.

8. Charles Dickens Museum, WC1

Explore the life of Charles Dickens via the restored rooms of the only home he lived in that is still standing. The museum hosts temporary exhibitions about his writing and Victorian London.

9. The Charterhouse, EC1

One of the most respected monasteries in London. Founded on the site of a former plaque pit in the 14th century, it has served as a Tudor mansion, a school and a charitable almshouse, and is still home to around 50 residents today.

10. London Mithraeum, EC4

Ruins of the Roman Temple of Mithras have been restored in their original location under Bloomberg's European HQ. Descend into the basement to enjoy an immersive experience that takes you back into the city 2,000 years ago.

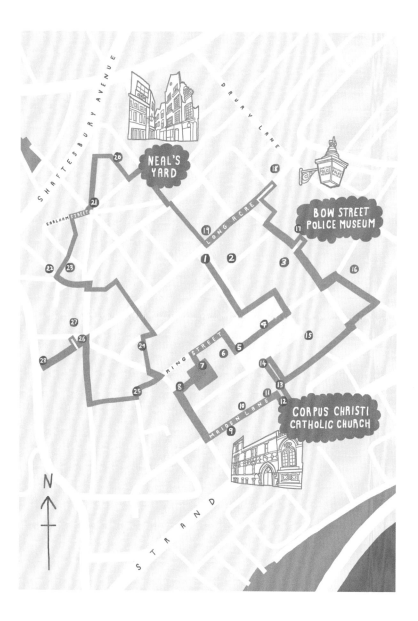

Covent Garden walk

START
Covent Garden
London Underground
Station

FINISH
Leicester Square
London Underground
Station

DISTANCE
2.8km (1.7 miles)

Situated in the heart of London's West End, Covent Garden is a tourist hotspot, known for its vibrant Piazza which hosts a market and eclectic street performers.

The surrounding area is full of shops, restaurants and theatres, however if not purposely visiting these, Londoners often tend to avoid the area. But this shouldn't be the case! Covent Garden is packed with history and hidden details as well as a host of theatrical characters and dramatic events – both onstage and off – that have left their mark on the area.

Opposite Covent Garden Market
Below Bridge of Aspiration

The walk starts at Covent Garden Station, one of the earlier stations on the London Underground network, having opened in 1907, and clad in the characteristic oxblood tiles of architect Leslie Green ❶ Do you feel a presence nearby? It is said that the ghost of an actor haunts the station – you shall meet him again later on. **From the station, follow James Street towards Covent Garden Market.**

Pause briefly to look up to the left along Floral Street, where you can admire a striking glass-and-steel walkway between two buildings ❷ This is the Bridge of Aspiration, designed by WilkinsonEyre and completed in 2003. It connects the Royal Ballet School with the Royal Opera House and, if you are lucky, you can occasionally see tutu-clad dancers walking across the bridge. **As you enter Covent Garden Market, turn left under the colonnade and stop here to read some history.**

Until the 1500s the land here was owned by Westminster Abbey – its name is actually a corruption of 'convent gardens'. The earliest development started when the land passed into the hands of the 1st Earl of Bedford, John Russell. King Henry VIII (r. 1509–47) gifted him the monastic land and the Bedford Estate still owns huge swathes of Covent Garden and

Bloomsbury today. You will encounter reminders of this throughout your walk. Covent Garden as we know it started to take shape under the 4th Earl of Bedford, Francis Russell, who inherited the estate in 1619. The stage was set for London's first attempt at town planning.

Between 1629 and 1637 work was underway as part of a team effort from King Charles I (r. 1625–49), Francis Russell and the architect Inigo Jones. Together they created an extraordinary new scene in London:

an open public place known as the Piazza, surrounded by fine houses, intended as a new aristocratic suburb. However, Covent Garden only enjoyed a short time as London's most desirable new neighbourhood, the popularity of the fruit and vegetable market ultimately leading to less salubrious businesses and residents.

The market was officially founded by royal charter in 1670, but trading had taken place since 1649. Not best pleased to be sharing an address with tradesmen, owners started moving further west or north and the surrounding buildings were used as coffeehouses, taverns and brothels, further damaging the respectability of the place. One of the most famous

taverns was the Shakespeare's Head, which stood at the northeast corner of the Piazza, roughly on the site of the entrance of the Royal Opera House, the rear of which you can see ahead ❸ The chief waiter was a man called Jack Harris, known as the 'Pimp General', the go-to source for the best available women. Trading off Harris's fame, in 1757, the writer Samuel Derrick published a book called *Harris's List of Covent Garden Ladies*, which detailed the location, price and sexual specialities of women in the West End. During the 18th century Covent Garden was colloquially known as the 'Square of Venus'.

The fruit, vegetable and flower market finally moved out of the area

Opposite Covent Garden Station
Right Punch & Judy pub

in November 1974 and survives as New Covent Garden in Nine Elms, Wandsworth. Today no houses from Inigo Jones's original plan survive, but there are some earlier buildings, which you will see shortly.

Take a stroll through the North Hall and Apple Market ❹ The market buildings date from 1828–30 and were designed by architect Charles Fowler. Today they host a mix of cafes, restaurants, high-end chain stores and boutiques, as well as some stalls reserved for independent artists and designers. On exiting the market buildings you are met with the impressive facade of St Paul's Covent Garden. This is the only existing part of Inigo Jones's original, dating from 1631–8 but restored in the 1800s following a fire in 1795.

Perhaps a dominating sight today, the church was actually something of an afterthought. According to Horace Walpole, writing in 1765, the Earl of Bedford asked Inigo Jones for a church in Covent Garden but said 'he wou'd not go to any considerable expence; in short, said he, I wou'd not have it much better than a barn.—Well then, replied Jones, you shall have the handsomest barn in England.'

At first glance you might assume that this is the front entrance of the church, but look closer and you will

see the space reserved for a central door is blocked off. This is the east end of the church, traditionally where the altar is placed. William Prynne, writing in the 17th century, explained that church authorities weren't happy with breaking conventional positioning and so Jones was pressured to change his design. Whether or not this is true, today we are left with a church that is the 'wrong' way round.

Look up to the left-hand side of the church and you will see an inscription in the stonework ❺ This records that, in 1662, Samuel Pepys witnessed a performance of Punch's Puppet Show here, now better known as Punch and Judy, and is a reminder of the long history of public performance in this

space. Glance behind you, and you will also spot the Punch & Judy pub which provides an excellent drinking terrace for watching the eclectic mix of street entertainers below.

Exit to the right of the church, towards King Street. Laid out in 1633–7, this street gives you the best idea of the grand plans for Covent Garden. Ahead, at no. 43, is the oldest surviving house in the Piazza, dating from 1716–17 and built for Admiral Russell, younger son of the 4th Duke of Bedford, who lived (and died) here.

As you walk along King Street, keep your eyes peeled for a narrow entrance to St Paul's Churchyard on the left ❻ This lovely little green space provides an oasis of calm in contrast to the bustling Piazza, and it is from here that you can see the true entrance into St Paul's Church ❼ If open, it is worth going inside and admiring some of the memorials. Given its proximity to London's theatreland, it is perhaps unsurprising that it is known as the 'actor's' church and contains the ashes of Dame Ellen Terry along with dedications

Opposite (far left) St Paul's Church;
(left) Bedford family crest;
(bottom) Eamonn Hughes's sculpture

to Charlie Chaplin, Noël Coward and Vivien Leigh. On the right-hand wall is a memorial to Charles Macklin, an 18th-century actor who regularly performed at the Theatre Royal Drury Lane (seen later on the walk) and who was celebrated for bringing more natural performances into the limelight – a technique you might describe as 'method acting' today. Macklin had a dramatic life offstage, and in 1735 he got into a fight with fellow actor Thomas Hallam. During the altercation Macklin managed to stab Hallam through the eye, killing him. He was tried for murder but sentenced only to manslaughter. Macklin lived to the age of 97 and the theatrical mask with a knife through the eye on his memorial is surely a reference to this violent incident.

Follow the map to exit St Paul's Churchyard onto Bedford Street. Look up as you pass through the iron gates to see the three scallops and rampart (upright) red lion of the Bedford family crest **8**

Turn left along Bedford Street and then left again along Maiden Lane. Given that this area was the centre of the 18th-century sex trade, you could be forgiven for assuming Maiden Lane was a reference to young, attractive women. However, there are two conflicting theories on the name –

neither of which is bawdy. The first is that the name is derived from a statue of the Virgin Mary that used to stand on the street. The second, that it is a corruption of the Old English *midden* meaning 'dung heap'! The latter might be the better fit as Maiden Lane, as well as Floral Street to the north, are London's first mews streets – service streets that housed stables for the smarter homes fronting Covent Garden Piazza.

Look up above The Porterhouse pub to spot a blue plaque dedicated to the painter JMW Turner, who was born in a house on this site in 1775. On an artistic theme, just beyond the pub, in Exchange Court, you will see a curious sculpture – a kind of three-dimensional architectural sketch – by Eamonn Hughes that was unveiled in 1998. It has a wonderful detail of women dashing from between the columns of a portico.

Back on Maiden Lane is the stage door of the Adelphi Theatre, which first opened in 1806 **9** It was here – as the nearby green plaque shares – that actor William Terriss met his untimely death in 1897. A popular Victorian actor, Terriss was praised for his good looks and charisma; his murderer was Richard Prince, a fellow actor with whom Terriss had previously worked. Prince was known to be

mentally unstable and apparently held a grudge against Terriss. Having fatally stabbed Terriss three times, Prince was sentenced to life imprisonment at Broadmoor Criminal Lunatic Asylum rather than face death by hanging. Terriss's ghost is said to haunt the theatre as well as Covent Garden Station, which occupies the site of a bakery that he used to frequent.

On the other side of the street, at nos 34 and 35, you can see the attractive facade of Rules, celebrated as London's oldest restaurant **10** Supposedly founded by a Thomas Rule, an oyster seller on Maiden Lane in 1798, the first concrete piece of evidence for the establishment comes with Benjamin Rule, who ran a fishmonger's on Maiden Lane and appears as a ratepayer in 1828. Benjamin moved into no. 35 in 1873 and the building retains its original brick frontage from this time. The restaurant later expanded next door into what was previously a (less appetizing) chemical apparatus maker.

Towards the end of Maiden Lane, you might be surprised to find a rather large Catholic church, Corpus Christi **11** It was granted a lease by the Bedford Estate in 1873 and the church was completed a year later. If it is open, do pop inside to admire the decorated interior. At the end of

Opposite (top) Corpus Christi; **(centre)** Ambrose Godfrey plaque; **(bottom)** Working donkeys of Covent Garden

Maiden Lane is Southampton Street, which ploughs through what would have been Bedford House, the mansion on the Strand owned by the Russell family mentioned earlier. The house, once a rural retreat, was demolished in the early 1700s as London grew around it, making it far too tempting to sell for a tidy profit. The name Southampton is from the 4th Earl of Southampton, whose daughter married into the Russell family in 1669.

Look out for the green plaque on the corner building of Southampton Street and Maiden Lane ⑫ It recalls that Ambrose Godfrey, the German-born chemist, lived and worked here from 1706–41. Godfrey arrived in London in 1679, first working under Robert Boyle before setting up his own shop selling phosphorus. Although the Bedford Estate banned the production of noxious trade (any businesses emitting foul-smelling or polluting by-products), Godfrey found a loophole by using a strip of land behind his shop in Maiden Lane where he also demonstrated scientific experiments. He is also credited with inventing the fire extinguisher in the 1720s.

Follow the map up Southampton Street. Nos 26 and 27 are rare survivors from the early 1700s, a glimpse of domestic architecture built in the decades following the Great Fire of London ⑬ From 1749, as the plaque here indicates, it was home to the actor David Garrick. Garrick was a friend and student of Charles Macklin, adopting the new, naturalistic style of acting, and became one of the most famous actors of his day. From 1747–76 he successfully managed the Theatre Royal Drury Lane and is buried in Poets' Corner, Westminster Abbey.

For a more unsung hero of the area, head to the top of Southampton Street and the corner of Jubilee Market Hall, built as the Foreign Flower Market in 1904. You will see a plaque commemorating the working donkeys of Covent Garden Market ⑭ Henry Mayhew, a journalist and social researcher who wrote *London Labour and the London Poor* (1851), recorded that on any given Saturday as many as 2,000 donkey-barrows could be seen, and vividly describes the market in full swing: 'From Long Acre to the Strand on the one side, and from Bow-street to Bedford-street on the other, the ground has been seized upon by the market-goers. As you glance down any one of the neighbouring streets, the long rows of carts and donkey-barrows seem interminable in the distance . . . Nothing is to be seen, on all sides, but vegetables; the pavement is covered with heaps of them waiting to be carted; the

flag-stones are stained green with the leaves trodden under foot; sieves and sacks full of apples and potatoes, and bundles of broccoli and rhubarb, are left unwatched upon almost every door-step; the steps of Covent Garden Theatre are covered with fruit and vegetables; the road is blocked up with mountains of cabbages and turnips; and men and women push past with their arms bowed out by the cauliflowers under them, or the red tips of carrots pointing from their crammed aprons.'

Retrace your steps down Southampton Street to turn left along Tavistock Street. You will pass behind the redbrick and green ironwork of the London Transport Museum ⓯ The building was the former flower market, built 1871–7, and was converted into a museum in the late 1970s.

Cross Wellington Street to stay on Tavistock Street and then turn left up Catherine Street until you reach Theatre Royal Drury Lane ⓰ This is the oldest surviving theatre in London, but there have been many different buildings on this site. The earliest theatre was a temporary affair dating from the 1630s, while the first permanent building was erected in 1662–3 and granted a patent by King Charles II – hence the 'royal' in its

name. That theatre burned down in 1672, as did its successor. In 1775 David Garrick employed Robert Adam to build a grander building, itself soon replaced by an even grander building in the 1790s under then theatre-manager Richard Brinsley Sheridan. It shouldn't come as too much of a surprise that, in 1809, this also burned down and the building seen today dates from 1810–12. Needless to say, they take fire safety very seriously.

At the end of Catherine Street, turn left and then right into Bow Street. Here, you see the other major theatrical venue in Covent Garden, the Royal Opera House, this time from the front. The current theatre dates from 1858, but there have been

three previous theatres here since 1732. From this viewpoint, the real star is the arched glass-and-iron Paul Hamlyn Hall, also from 1858. Formerly called the Floral Hall, it was designed by Edward Barry, son of the more famous Charles Barry. As the name suggests it was intended to house exotic flowers, fruits and vegetables and provide some extra income for the Opera House. But when the Duke of Bedford opened a rival flower market (already seen, and now housing the London Transport Museum), it only lasted for a few years before it was transformed into a concert hall and occasional ice rink. The hall became part of Covent Garden Market in 1887 but lay derelict after a fire in the 1950s.

The Royal Opera House bought it back in 1977, using it to store scenery until a refurbishment in the 1990s saw it restored to become this dazzling events space, cafe and bar.

Almost directly opposite is the sign for the Bow Street Police Museum on Martlett Court **17** The museum first opened it doors in 2021 and stands within the old Bow Street police station, one of the earliest stations in London, and which closed in 1992 (see also, page 77).

The Metropolitan Police was founded in 1829 by Sir Robert Peel. Prior to that an organization existed, known as the Bow Street Runners. From 1740 a local magistrate, Thomas de Veil, ran a court from his home at no. 4 Bow Street. He passed the proverbial police baton to Henry Fielding, the novelist, and a fellow magistrate, who established a local team of men to catch London's criminals. The Runners worked independently until they merged with the Metropolitan Police in 1837.

Look above the door to the museum and you will see small rectangular windows set into the wall. These are the original police cells and now form part of the museum's exhibition space. The police station was also attached to the Bow Street Magistrates Court, now a hotel, although the Grade II listed building (1879–80, by Sir John Taylor) retains a few details, such as the crown-topped lamps and lettering along the facade. The magistrates court heard some of the most famous trials of the 19th and early 20th centuries, from that of East End gangsters and convicted murderers, the Kray twins, to Oscar Wilde's trial for gross indecency in 1895, and from the trial of Dr Crippen, who murdered his wife Cora and buried her under the basement of their house, to that of Sylvia and Christabel Pankhurst, charged with breach of the peace in 1908 while protesting for the vote for women.

Further along Bow Street, turn right onto Broad Court. Here, you can see a much-photographed line of red telephone boxes, to which journalists would dash out and report back verdicts to their newspaper offices. **Turn left, still on Broad Court, and then right onto Long Acre.** Looming ahead is the stone Freemason's Hall, the central headquarters of English freemasonry. The current building dates from 1927–33, but there has been a freemason's hall here since the 1770s. Today they arrange regular tours of the building and have a small museum open to the public.

At no. 69 Long Acre, look up above Brompton Cycles to see that, in a twist of fate, this is actually the home of cycling, where Britain's first bicycle was sold in 1819 **18** The peddle-less 'hobby horse' design was patented a year earlier by Denis Johnson, a coachmaker who had a shop here.

Retrace your steps along Long Acre, and continue down the street until you reach the corner of Neal Street **19** The curious female figure looking down at you has a history dating back to 1510, the year the Lord Mayor Thomas Bradbury died and his wealthy widow, Joan, began buying farmland in Marylebone, St Giles and Covent Garden. When she died in 1530, she left the 149 acres to the Mercers' Company (see page 34). Originally Joan Bradbury had intended

Left (top) Mercers' Maiden, Neal Street;
(bottom) Neal's Yard

to create a chantry chapel to her late husband (a place in which prayers could be said for him to speed him through purgatory). However, since this Catholic ritual was banned in 1547, her whole estate was seized by the Crown. Eventually the Mercers' Company paid a fine to keep the land. A savvy move, as today they still own five acres of land across Covent Garden, the income from which has bolstered their charitable foundation for almost 500 years. The female figure looking down from the corner of Neal Street is a Mercers' Maiden – the symbol of the company, which can also be seen on the black street bollards nearby. Keep your eyes peeled in the vicinity for more maidens, a sign that a building is owned by the Mercers' Company.

Continue up Neal Street, passing the attractive Edwardian pub, the Crown & Anchor, and turn left up Short's Gardens. Look up to the right to see a curious clock on the side of the building, which collects rainwater in the clear tube. The clock was installed in 1982 by Tim Hunkin and Andy Plant. On the hour the figures below the clockface used to move, with water filtering into the flower beds below through the watering cans – on occasion an unlucky passerby could be drenched by an overhanging

spout! Sadly, it no longer works today. The clock was once part of Neal's Yard Wholefood Warehouse, which is where you are heading next. **Almost immediately, turn right onto the narrow Neal's Yard to emerge into a tiny, colourful courtyard 20**

In 1976 Nicholas Saunders moved into 2 Neal's Yard, buying the warehouse for £2,000 and opening a wholefood shop. Saunders was an activist and part of the alternative movement in the 1970s. He published advice for young Londoners on squatting, living communally and cheaply, as well as DIY and legal advice. His shop was a huge success, an embodiment of his ideals of a caring capitalist hub that promoted fair-trade and eco-friendly practices. Saunders expanded into a dairy and apothecary (now Neal's Yard Remedies).

Follow Neal's Yard, passing through Seven Dials Court, to exit on Monmouth Street. Ahead is a redbrick building that is now a hotel. Look up to admire the lettering that tells you that this was once the French hospital and dispensary that opened in 1890 with 60 patient beds. This was the second French hospital in the area, established with the aim of providing foreigners with medical relief. The first opened in 1867 near Leicester Square, later expanding to this site.

The hospital closed in the 1960s.

Turn left onto Monmouth Street, at the end of which you will arrive at Seven Dials 21 Seven Dials was part of the property of Westminster Abbey given to King Henry VIII and in the 1500s was simply referred to as marshland. By 1650 there was a scattered collection of brick inns, industrial sites and some wood-and-thatched homes, and it wasn't until 1693 that things picked up pace. The Member of Parliament Thomas Neale bought a lease to the site, intent on improving the area and turning a profit. To do so, he wanted to maximize rent by creating the largest shop frontages possible, hence the seven streets radiating out like spokes

Right The Ivy

of a wheel. If you look up to the top of the column in the centre however, you will notice that there are only six sun dials. One theory is that the original street plan only included six streets, another is that the column itself is intended as the seventh sundial.

Unfortunately, Neale's grand plan for creating a retail hub was unsuccessful and over the next decades the area descended into slums. In 1836 Charles Dickens, writing in *Sketches by Boz*, described Seven Dials as: 'The streets and courts dart in all directions, until they are lost in the unwholesome vapour which hangs over the house-tops, and renders the dirty perspective uncertain and confined; and lounging at every corner, as if they came there to take a few gasps of such fresh air as has found its way so far, but is too much exhausted already, to be enabled to force itself into the narrow alleys around, are groups of people, whose appearance and dwellings would fill any mind but a regular Londoner's with astonishment.'

Follow the map via Earlham Street and turning left down the narrow Tower Court. This gives you an insight into the higgledy-piggledy alleys and decrepit housing that used to make up this area. **As you emerge from Tower Court onto West Street,** directly

ahead is The Ivy ㉒ Established in 1917, this restaurant immediately appealed to the local theatrical neighbourhood, who could enjoy delicious food and a gossip behind the colourful stained-glass windows. This is the original branch of the restaurant, but its exclusive image has been somewhat tarnished by an ever-increasing number of franchises across the UK.

On the opposite side of West Street is the home of the world's longest running play: Agatha Christie's *The Mousetrap*, which had its world premiere on 6 October 1952 before opening in London in November ㉓ It has been at St Martin's Theatre since 1974 and has broken every record for longevity in the history of the theatre.

Walk past the theatre to follow West Street to where it crosses Upper St Martin's Lane and head down Slingsby Place. The name is a reference to William Slingsby who developed the land in the 17th century. Today it is a modern network of retail and commercial units. Cross Long Acre – remembering to look up for Mercers' Maidens overhead – and follow the map through Conduit Court and onto Floral Street. Ahead to the right is the wonderfully atmospheric Lazenby Court, laid out around 1688, which leads to the Lamb & Flag pub ❷❹ It claims to have been established in 1623, but the house was rebuilt in 1688 and most of the building dates from the early 18th

century. The building only became a pub in 1772 and the frontage was replaced in the 1950s, however it is still a great place to have a drink. Claims that bare-knuckle boxing fights were held in the upstairs rooms during the 19th century have led to it being nicknamed the delightfully sounding 'bucket of blood'.

Leave the Lamb & Flag via Rose Street, to emerge on Garrick Street. Walk on past the Round House pub into New Row, then turn left into Bedfordbury. Almost immediately, look out for the tiny entrance on the right into Goodwin's Court ❷❺ Laid out in 1690, and originally called Fisher's Alley, the shop fronts here date from the late 18th century and there

Opposite (left) St Martin's Theatre;
(right) Goodwin's Court **Right (top)**
Agatha Christie memorial; **(bottom)**
4 Great Newport Street

are original mid-19th-century gas lamps, all contributing to one of the loveliest little alleys in the West End. **As you exit onto St Martin's Lane, turn right and walk up towards the traffic interchange.** On the corner of Cranbourn Street and Great Newport Street is a memorial to Agatha Christie ❷❻ Unveiled in 2012 and designed by Ben Twiston Davies, a bust of Christie sits within a book decorated with images of characters and scenes from her novels.

Your last stop on this walk is something of an enigma, and hard to spot unless you know what you are looking for. **Cross over towards the black-tiled building at no. 4 Great Newport Street.** Look closely at the facade, and you will see a hook labelled 'Metropolitan Police' ❷❼ As so often with London stories, it is very hard to wheedle out the truth of oddities such as this, but you may read that this was a hook used by policemen in the early 20th century for hanging up their coats in hot weather while directing traffic. Whatever the reason, this is a delightful curiosity to admire as you walk by. **Return to Cranbourn Street and follow the map to reach Leicester Square Station, where the walk ends** ❷❽

IN FOCUS • BOUNDARY MARKERS

Once you start looking, you will notice that London is full of markers that indicate distances, boundaries and property ownership.

LET'S TAKE A CLOSER LOOK

The most straightforward of these markers are milestones letting you know the distance from a specific location or just Central London. The official centre of London is just south of Trafalgar Square, specifically the equestrian statue of King Charles I (r. 1625–49). The statue dates from 1633 and replaced a far earlier marker known as an Eleanor Cross, erected in accordance with stops made by the funeral cortège of Queen Eleanor, wife of King Edward I (r. 1272–1307). Confusingly, a replica Eleanor Cross stands outside Charing Cross Station today, but the next time you see a '10 miles to London' sign, it is 16km (10 miles) to this exact point, the statue of King Charles I.

Parish boundary markers
Some markers are less easy to fathom, for example, the odd plaques that can be seen on walls. These are parish boundary markers. The parish was the community living around a particular church, which organized local services prior to there being a centralized government in London (only

established with the Local Government Act of 1899, which created the Metropolitan Boroughs of London). Parishes had responsibilities such as collecting taxes, maintaining roads, organizing local security and looking after the poor. Given these duties, it was important to know exactly who was responsible for what and so physical markers were installed to remind residents and to settle any disputes.

Sometimes it is easy to match the initials of these metal plates with nearby churches, but in some cases the church has since been demolished, making a marker harder to identify. Although they are now defunct, there has never been much cause to take them all down and so they can still be widely spotted across London on buildings pre-dating 1899. They're also occasionally reinstalled on modern buildings for their historical interest.

Wards and boroughs

Other markers you might see denote different wards or boroughs. Ward markers can be found exclusively within the City of London, which is still

Opposite Parish boundary markers
Above (top) St George's Circus mile marker, Southwark; **(bottom)** Old and new borough signs

comprised of 25 wards, each electing common councillors and aldermen to represent the interests of the local businesses and residents.

Indicators of boroughs can be found all over Greater London, mainly along the bottom of street signs. Modern signs (dating from after 1965) will show one of the 33 London boroughs (including the City) but sometimes you can see older street signs that reference the earlier boroughs that existed between 1899 and 1965.

Dragons

Dragon markers symbolize the City of London and announce its boundaries along major thoroughfares. Besides a very fearsome-looking dragon outside the Royal Courts of Justice on the Strand, there are more heraldic silver dragons dotted around the City's perimeter (see page 29).

Opposite (top) Temple Bar memorial dragon;
(bottom) Drapers' Company coat of arms

Fire plugs

You will find it difficult to match the initials 'F P' with any nearby church or area. This is because the two letters stand for Fire Plug and have nothing to do with boundaries. Instead, they mark places in the belowground water mains, where firefighters cut a small hole into the pipe in order to access water when dealing with a nearby fire. Plugging the hole once the fire is out, the firefighters then attached an F P plate so that the same hole could be used again, so saving time (and presumably too many leaky pipes) should another fire ever occur nearby.

The largest of these can be found along the Embankment and were originally decorative elements on the Coal Exchange which stood on Thames Street until 1962. The others are smaller replicas of this design and appear on Bishopsgate, Aldgate High Street, Tower Hill, Holborn, Farringdon Street and Goswell Road as well as at the southern ends of Blackfriars and London Bridges.

Livery companies
Also unique to the City are the property marks of livery companies, of which there are 110 representing various trades from clothmakers to fishmongers. Some of these companies have histories dating back to the 12th century, while others are modern, such as The Worshipful Company of Information Technologists, founded in 2010. Many own property within the City and further afield and mark their assets with a unique coat of arms. One of the most prevalent of these markers is the Mercers' Maiden (see pages 34 and 91).

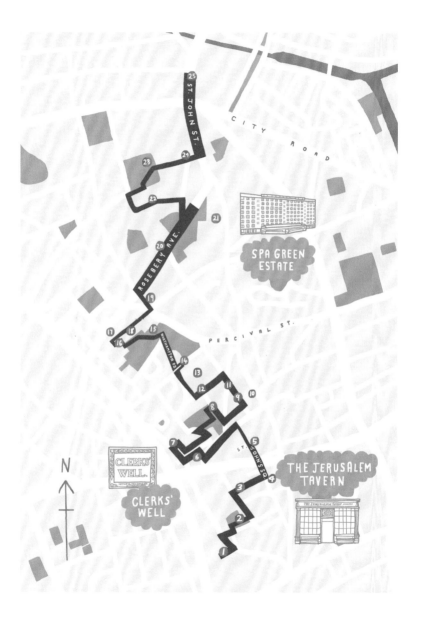

Clerkenwell walk

START
Farringdon London
Underground Station

FINISH
Angel London
Underground Station

DISTANCE
3.2km (2 miles)

For an area so close to central London, right on the edge of the City, Clerkenwell has a surprisingly quiet, neighbourhood feel. This is partly thanks to its strong links with religious settlements, a belt of monastic organizations that sprung up outside the City walls from medieval times.

This walk encounters a number of these former religious houses but also explores the more radical recent history – progressive housing and health schemes, entrepreneurial entertainment venues and pioneering infrastructure projects.

Opposite The Jerusalem Tavern
Right (top) Girdlers' Company crest;
(bottom) Mountford House

The walk starts outside Farringdon
Station ❶ **Head north on Turnmill
Street towards Benjamin Street.**
At the corner of Benjamin Street,
look up at the more modern building
on the right. Against the yellow
bricks you can see a black and gold
crest, part of the coat of arms of
the Girdlers' Company, one of the
110 livery companies of the City of
London (see also, page 28). These
began as medieval trade guilds but
grew into powerful and wealthy
companies whose presence can still
be seen across London today. The
Girdlers' Company has owned land
here since the 17th century and the
properties along Benjamin Street
make up around 15 percent of their
Central London portfolio. Historically
the company made girdles (belts) but
today – aside from presenting a girdle
to the monarch at their coronation
– they are not closely linked to their
trade. On this walk you will see
plenty of evidence of the historic land
ownership that continues to influence
how the area looks and feels today.

**A short way up Benjamin Street
you will reach St John's Garden ❷**
A pleasant and shady green space,
this is a former burial ground, once
connected to a 12th-century priory
church that you will see later on.
**Follow the map through St John's
Garden and exit onto Britton Street,
turning left.** The street is named after
the antiquary and author John Britton
who worked in a nearby pub, now
demolished, in the early 1800s.

After a short walk, look up to the
left to see the decorative panels along
the top of Mountford House. Today
this building serves as modern offices,
but the reliefs were salvaged from
the former Booth's Gin Distillery on
this site, demolished in 1978. They
depict gin production, from the early
stages of harvesting raw ingredients

Opposite Clerks' Well

to distilling, and were carved around 1903 by Frederick W Pomeroy.

On the other side of the street, at no. 55, stands The Jerusalem Tavern ❸ Although the building is genuinely from 1720, as the sign suggests, the shopfront dates from 1810 and there has only been a pub here since the 1990s. It is still a wonderful pub though. **Turn right to walk down the narrow St John's Path beside the pub, a reminder of the tiny network of alleys that would have abounded here in the 1700s.**

If you were to walk this path a few centuries earlier, you would be heading towards the inner precinct of the Knights Hospitaller, a religious order with its origins in 1080, Jerusalem, where a hospital was established to aid Christian pilgrims en route to the Holy Land. These Hospitallers morphed into a more military role after the conquest of Jerusalem during the First Crusade and by the 12th century were known as the Knights of the Order of St John. In 1144 they built a priory here as their English headquarters and shortly on the right, on arriving at St John's Square, you will see the great gatehouse of the priory, St John's Gate, rebuilt in 1504 ❹

Medieval Clerkenwell was home to multiple religious communities

who settled just outside of the City of London walls and, over centuries, amassed great power and wealth. The Order of St John built a large church, a hall and various gardens, as well as housing for servants and for leasing to external tenants. The order was dissolved by King Henry VIII (r. 1509–47) in 1540 and the buildings were gradually sold to various secular owners, including for use as offices of the Master of the Revels which licensed thirty of William Shakespeare's plays.

Incredibly, the Order of St John continues in some form today. In 1888 Queen Victoria (r. 1837–1901) granted the order a royal charter and it now operates as a charity known as St John Ambulance, providing first-aid services and training. It is possible to visit the Museum of the Order of St John and it organizes brilliant tours.

Follow the map to continue on St John's Square, heading away from St John's Gate. Before crossing Clerkenwell Road look up at the yellow-brick building on the right-hand corner of St John's Square. The line of terracotta tiles above the first-floor windows tells you that this was a former Penny Bank. Built in 1880 this was the second branch of the National Penny Bank, a philanthropic society established in 1859 to provide housing,

shops and a bank. Its aim was to encourage the working classes to save money, accepting far smaller deposits than other banks. Unfortunately, it was a short-lived experiment and only lasted until 1914.

Cross Clerkenwell Road, constructed in the 1870s, which cleaves the medieval priory land in two. Here you can find the remains of St John Priory Church and Garden which, if the gates are open, is a wonderful place to have a sit down and soak up the peaceful atmosphere and fragrance of medicinal herbs ❺ Although the church retains its medieval crypt, the majority of what stands here was rebuilt after the Second World War. In the public square leading up to the gardens, look down at the pavement and you will see the curved path of stones that shows the line of the original church from 1144, burned down during the Peasants' Revolt of 1381.

Just beyond the priory, continue straight ahead on the pedestrianized Jerusalem Passage. This is the site of the postern gate and northernmost edge of the land owned by the Order of St John. At the end of the passage, look up to the right to see a green plaque remembering Thomas Britton. An English coal merchant by trade, Britton found fame as a singer and established a minuscule concert venue in the loft of his Clerkenwell home here from 1678 until the early 1700s.

Right St James Clerkenwell

Turn left to follow Aylesbury Street into Clerkenwell Green. At its heart, at no. 22, stands Middlesex Sessions House ❻ This once acted as the court house where criminal cases were heard before justices of the peace. It was built in 1778-82 and served as the main administrative centre for Middlesex until the creation of the County of London in 1889. This meant that Clerkenwell was now part of the London Metropolitan Borough of Finsbury, rather than Middlesex. On both the Clerkenwell Green and Farringdon Lane facade, above the red doors, you can see a surviving shield of Middlesex – three curved swords. It closed for judicial business in the early 1900s and since then has been used as a scales manufacturer and – intriguingly – The London Masonic Centre. As of 2021 it's been extensively refurbished, making the most of its grand, 18th-century interiors. You can get a feel for the space by visiting the restaurant, Sessions Arts Club.

You have already visited the grounds of one of the religious orders that dominated this area, but if you continue right on Farringdon Lane you will find the earliest surviving fragment of another. At nos 14–16 stands Well Court, a rather unattractive 1920s office block.

Between the pink stone pillars are some tinted windows and if you peer down through the glass, you will see a circular well, dating from around 1174. This was once part of St Mary's Priory, an Augustinian nunnery that was disbanded in 1539, and is in fact the Clerks' Well that gives the area its name ❼ Rather than an administrative role, as we might understand it today, 'clerk' in this context is a corruption of 'clerici', meaning clergy. This site was a popular place for medieval mystery plays and open-air performances of biblical stories. The well was closed after fears of contamination in 1857 and only rediscovered in the 1920s.

Return to Clerkenwell Green towards Clerkenwell Close. You will

Right The Sekforde

pass the Marx Memorial Library, at no. 37a, on your left. One of the older buildings on the green, although much restored, it was erected in 1738 as a Welsh school with the aim of providing an education to impoverished Welsh children of London. From the early 1900s it became a printing press for socialist publications and was where Vladimir Lenin would edit and print his paper *Iskra* (*The Spark*) from 1902–03. The building became the Marx Memorial Library in the 1930s. Continuing this radical theme, up ahead, The Crown Tavern is supposedly where Lenin first met Joseph Stalin in 1905.

Turn left up Clerkenwell Close and admire the fine view of St James Clerkenwell ❽ It stands on the former site of St Mary's Priory whose well you have just seen. The current church was built in the 1790s and designed by James Carr. If open, it is well worth looking inside. Pause in the entrance hall to admire a rare surviving modesty rail on the stairs, preventing those standing below from gazing up the skirts of women ascending to the church's galleries!

Once you have visited the church, exit the churchyard, turning right onto St James's Walk and crossing Sekforde Street to walk along Hayward's Place. You will pass the Woodbridge Chapel on your left, built in 1833 and home to the Clerkenwell and Islington Medical Mission ❾ **Before turning left onto Woodbridge Street, take a short detour a little way up Hayward's Place to get a closer look at the modern green plaque on the houses up ahead** ❿ It remembers the Red Bull Playhouse which, from 1605 until 1665, hosted theatrical performances, defiantly continuing even when ordered to close by the Puritans in 1642. Samuel Pepys visited in 1661 and wasn't too impressed, remarking in his diary that the play was poorly done; 'and with so much disorder, among others, in the musique-room, the boy that was to sing a song, not singing it right, his

Left Hugh Myddelton School

master fell about his eares and beat him so, that it put the whole house into an uprore'.

Back on Woodbridge Street, the pub occupying the attractive corner plot at the top of the street is The Sekforde ⑪ The name is a reference to the 16th-century lawyer Thomas Sekforde, who purchased part of the St Mary's Priory land after its dissolution. **Continue a short way on Woodbridge Street before turning left onto Sans Walk.** Embedded in the brickwork on your left is a plaque that informs you that this wall is the property of the County of Middlesex ⑫ As you saw with Old Sessions House earlier, this is a reminder that, until 1900, when it was absorbed into the London Metropolitan Borough of Finsbury, Clerkenwell was part of Middlesex. The name 'Sans' is also worth a mention: nothing to do with the French for 'without' but rather a reference to a Mr Edward Sans who, in 1893, was the oldest member of the local parish vestry and had the street named after him.

As you walk along Sans Walk and then bear right towards Clerkenwell Close, you are tracing the outer walls of the former Clerkenwell Prison. Today the space is occupied by Kingsway Place flats, renovated within the Victorian redbrick buildings that were once the Hugh Myddelton School ⑬ You will discover more about Myddelton later on. **As you follow the outer wall along Clerkenwell Close, turn right to walk a short distance on Corporation Row.** Here you will see former school entrances in the wall, each marked with a name like 'schoolkeeper', 'cookery and laundry' or 'girls and infants'. Corporation Row, itself, is the far wall of the former prison site ⑭ The first prison on this site was built in 1615 under the direction of the Middlesex justices of the peace. When it burned down in 1679 the prisoners were sent into the workhouse next door. It wasn't until the 1770s that a new, larger prison

Left The Exmouth Arms

solid alibi and consistent protests of innocence, he became the last person to be publicly hanged in England, outside Newgate Prison on 26 May 1868. The House of Detention finally closed in the 1880s.

Retrace your steps and continue along Northampton Road, passing the London Metropolitan Archives on your left. These house original documents, maps and letters relating to the history of London; their earliest item is a charter from King William I (r. 1066–87) dating from 1067. **Follow the map through Spa Fields, formerly known as Ducking-Pond Fields** ⓯ Reputedly a rough patch of land during the 17th and 18th centuries, this was once plagued by pickpockets after dark. Despite this, Spa Fields was a popular recreation space in the 1770s boasting such attractions as skittles, food and drink stalls, theatrical performances and even donkey races. It was also used as a burial ground, with an estimated 80,000 interments throughout its history. By the 1840s overcrowding of the site was such that gravediggers were removing old bodies nightly in order to make way for the new ones that would arrive the next day, and conditions started to cause public health concerns. After several scandalized news reports it finally closed to burials in 1853.

was built, only to be replaced again by an even larger and more modern building in the 1840s.

The House of Detention, as it became known, was for those awaiting trial for petty crimes, and on 13 December 1867 it was the site of a huge explosion as part of an attempted prison break. The plotters – a group of Irish Republicans – left a barrel of gunpowder alongside the outer wall (today's Corporation Row), blowing up an 18-m (60-ft) stretch of it. Reports vary, but around a dozen people died and around 100 were injured. Although several men were put on trial following the attack, only one was found guilty. His name was Michael Barrett and despite a

Right Finsbury Town Hall

Exit Spa Fields via Spa Fields Lane, to enter Exmouth Market. It is named after Admiral Edward Pellew, a British naval officer who was made 1st Viscount Exmouth after rescuing 1,000 Christian slaves from Algiers in 1816. This was a working-class street market from the 1890s but regeneration has seen it transformed into a popular destination with plenty of independent pubs, restaurants and shops. On your left as you exit Spa Fields Lane is the huge Italianate Church of Our Most Holy Redeemer, built in the 19th century ⑯ Opposite you will find the Exmouth Arms pub, which is a good break point if you are hungry or thirsty ⑰ Along the street at no. 56, look up to spot one of London's more unusual blue plaques ⑱ Joseph Grimaldi was a dancer, comedian and actor who developed the clown role of the pantomime to such an extent that it became known as 'Joey' after him. He lived at this address for 10 years until 1828 and regularly performed at Sadler's Wells Theatre which you will see shortly.

Coming out of Exmouth Market, cross Tysoe Street to enter Rosoman Street. Stop to admire the architectural details of Finsbury Town Hall, built in 1895 ⑲ Used for the borough of Finsbury until 1965 (when Finsbury became part of the new London borough of Islington), it hosted political meetings and events in its lavish interiors. Following years of decline it was thankfully restored in the early 2000s and now houses a community centre and dance school. As you make your way around the building and onto Rosebery Avenue, look out for the green plaque that commemorates Dadabhai Naoroji, Britain's first Asian MP, winning the Finsbury Central seat for the Liberal Party in 1892.

Continue up Rosebery Avenue. Along with Clerkenwell Road, this was one of the new roads built in the late 1800s by the Metropolitan Board of Works in order to provide a better route between Holborn and Angel.

A prettier reminder of town planning and infrastructure can be found ahead on the corner of Rosebery Avenue and Hardwick Street. **Cross the road to get a closer look.** This building is the former New River Head, now converted into flats, but previously the headquarters of the Metropolitan Water Board (MWB) whose initials you can see decorating the front doors **20** The MWB took over control from the New River Company in 1904, but the history of establishing clean water in this area goes back 300 years earlier to Edmund Colthurst.

Colthurst had a grand idea to dig a channel to bring water from Chadwell Springs, Hertfordshire, into London, in 1604. However, the project ran out of money and so, in 1609, Hugh Myddelton – an MP and successful goldsmith – took over, completing the New River in 1613 and taking all the glory. You saw the former school named after him earlier. This building is just one part of a huge site that once housed a reservoir, providing Londoners with fresh water. Today what remains of the New River is managed by Thames Water. Ahead is another part of the New River Head complex, the Laboratory Building. Built in the 1930s, it originally contained a laboratory, research centre and offices, and is now home to 35 flats.

On the other side of Rosebery Avenue is another residential project, the Spa Green Estate **21** **You may want to cross over into Spa Green Garden to get a better view.** This ambitious housing project was envisaged as a shining example of cutting-edge architecture, replacing slum housing with a practical and desirable place to live. Finsbury Metropolitan Borough hired Georgia-born Russian architect Berthold Lubetkin in the late 1930s but, owing to disruption during the Second World War, the estate was not completed until 1949. Across three blocks Spa Green Estate housed 126 flats, all with an emphasis on light and ventilation and fitted with the latest central heating, bathrooms and kitchens. The estate received Grade II* listed status in 1998 and is still considered one of the best examples of council-funded housing in the country.

Cross back over the road to turn into Arlington Way. You will pass the modern Sadler's Wells Theatre on your right. The sixth building on this site today, this is a world-leading centre for dance, but it all began with the discovery of a mineral spring by Richard Sadler. In 1683 he developed a venue here and attracted crowds to the spring with various performances from singers, dancers, jugglers, wrestlers and, supposedly, a singing duck.

Right St Mark's Church

Turn left down the narrow Myddelton Passage 22 After a short walk, pay close attention to the brick wall. You will start to see letters and numbers roughly carved into the bricks. Right up until 2006 these carvings remained a mystery. But thanks to Peter Guillery from English Heritage and Margaret Bird of the Metropolitan Police Archive, the history began to unravel.

During the 19th century this was a dark, crime-ridden passageway and policemen – mainly from the 'G' (Finsbury) division of the Metropolitan Police – would walk through here on their regular beats. Over time these tired and bored policemen took to carving their uniform collar numbers into the bricks and that is what we can see today, with examples such as '234G' and '365PLYMOUTH'. Exit Myddelton Passage into Myddelton Square, the largest residential square in Clerkenwell 23 It was erected over 21 years by 13 different builders on behalf of the New River Estate, and completed in 1836. It was a respectable address, home to carpenters, watchmakers, teachers, merchants, architects and priests. At its centre is the impressive St Mark's Church, built 1825–7 and designed by architect and engineer William Chadwell Mylne. This was Mylne's sole ecclesiastical

project in his career and he overspent by £3,000.

Follow the map through the attractive gardens and exit the square via Chadwell Street. The name of the street is a reminder of the springs that feed the New River, and it was laid out in the 1820s–30s. Ahead, on the right, is an attractive late-19th-century shopfront with the signage of Thomas B. Treacy Funeral Directors, established in 1925 24 Thomas Treacy's second branch, on Rosebery Avenue, houses in its basement the very niche Museum of Funeral History, founded by employee and history lover Kelvin Sanderson. Sadly, Kelvin passed away in March 2021, but the museum is still open to visitors today, by prior appointment only.

Savour the last of the quiet, residential surroundings of Chadwell Street as you follow the map onto the busy St John Street, which becomes Islington High Street. It is then a short walk to Angel Station where the walk ends 25

TOP 10 · STATUES

Of the thousands of public statues to be found in London, here are a few of the more interesting ones to look out for.

1. Hodge, EC4
One of a surprising number of statues dedicated to cats. Hodge was the favourite pet cat of Dr Samuel Johnson, author of the *English Dictionary*. The statue stands outside his former home.

2. Royal Artillery War Memorial, W1
Created by Charles Sargeant Jagger, this war memorial is staggering for its realism. A huge, accurately carved howitzer gun towers over bronze sculptures that include an unconventional depiction of a dead soldier.

3. John Keats, Guys Hospital, SE1
Keats studied as an apothecary surgeon at Guy's Hospital for two years before becoming a poet. This statue is noteworthy for its base, a stone alcove that once stood on the Old London Bridge in the 1700s!

4. A Conversation with Oscar Wilde, WC2
Wilde was known for his intelligence and wit. With this sculpture by Maggi Hambling, you're encouraged to sit with Wilde and have a chat – his swirling smoky form looking as if he is just about to reply.

5. Gilt of Cain, EC3
Marking 200 years since the abolition of the slave trade, this ambiguous sculpture by Michael Visochi – does it depict a preacher's pulpit or a slave auction? – incorporates a Lemn Sissay poem that interweaves the horrors of the slave trade with the capitalist greed that fuelled it.

6. Millicent Garrett Fawcett, SW1
The first statue of a woman to grace Parliament Square, the 2018 carving by Gillian Wearing also includes various figures from the women's suffrage movement around its base.

7. Elizabeth I, EC4
One of the oldest public statues in London, this was carved in 1586, during the life of Queen Elizabeth I (r. 1558–1603). Originally it stood on Lud Gate, a City gateway that was torn down in 1760.

8. Kindertransport – The Arrival, EC2
This sculpture by Liverpool Street Station remembers the evacuation of Jewish children saved from the Nazis during the Second World War. The sculptor, Frank Miesler, was one of the 10,000 children that managed to escape by train and arrived here around 1938–9.

9. Street Art by Jonesy
Keep looking up in the East End and you might be rewarded with spying an artwork by Jonesy. These small bronze casts are often ethereal and almost always have an environmental message.

10. Women of World War II, SW1
Echoing the Cenotaph on Whitehall, this 2005 sculpture by John W. Mills commemorates the contribution of seven million women during the Second World War. The inscription is written in the typeface used in ration books and the 17 different uniforms symbolize the hundreds of roles that women filled.

Whitechapel walk

START
Aldgate East London
Underground Station

FINISH
Stepney Green
London Underground
Station

DISTANCE
3km (1.9 miles)

Between 1800 and 1900, London's population rose at an unprecedented rate, from around one million to almost six million people. In the poorest areas of London – including the East End – this meant more hungry mouths to feed, many people crowded into unsanitary rooms and less work to be found.

The area soon became associated with crime and poverty. Mention Whitechapel to anyone today and the likely first response is 'Oh, like Jack the Ripper?' However the murders of 1888 represent just a tiny part of Whitechapel's story. This walk uncovers the philanthropists, immigrants and professional men and women who have shaped the area's character today.

Right Gunthorpe Street

The walk starts at Aldgate East Station ❶ **If arriving by Tube, leave the station via exit 2, following the signs towards Petticoat Lane. Then turn left out of the station, crossing Commercial Street at the traffic lights and walking straight along Aldgate High Street until you reach the White Hart pub.**

Alongside the pub is the narrow alley of Gunthorpe Street ❷ It was renamed from George Yard in 1912, perhaps to downplay the notoriety of a murder that had taken place here in 1888. Martha Tabram was born Martha White in Southwark on 10 May 1849, and in many ways her life was typical of the harsh conditions and minimal prospects for East End women in the 19th century. Sometime after her father died (when she was 16) she began living with a man called Henry and by the time she was 20, the pair were married and went on to have two sons. Henry separated from Martha in 1875, blaming her heavy drinking, but with the lack of decent paid jobs for women, she still relied on him paying her 12 shillings a week. When he found out she was living with another man he cut this sum in half. Martha found her way to Whitechapel, drinking in the local taverns and as an occasional visitor to the workhouse. On 7 August 1888, aged 39, she was found dead in George Yard, with multiple stab wounds. Today she is a footnote in the story of Jack the Ripper, with those interested in finally unmasking the unknown serial killer debating whether she was or wasn't one of his victims. Perhaps we should remember her life and name instead?

The Whitechapel Murders of 1888 often spring to mind when considering this area of East London. They were sensational at the time and continue to attract macabre attention. Most streets associated with the murders and victims have either had their names changed or been obliterated as part of slum clearance plans, and yet the popularity of Jack the Ripper tours endures.

Whitechapel Gallery ❹ Opened in 1902, this and the library next door were part of a movement spearheaded by philanthropists to improve the lives of people living in the East End. The golden leaves were added by British artist Tracey Emin in 2012, as part of celebrations for London hosting the Olympic Games. You can also spot a large weathervane depicting a man riding a horse backwards, reading a book. This is in fact the Canadian artist of the piece, Rodney Graham, in the guise of the Dutch scholar Desiderius Erasmus, who, it is claimed, wrote his most famous work *The Praise of Folly* while on a horseback journey from Italy to England around 1510. The weathervane was installed in 2009.

Return to Whitechapel High Street. Look out for the ornate symbol above the entrance to Gunthorpe Street ❸ This is a reminder that the *Jewish Daily Post*, established in 1926, was based here until 1935. The sign was designed by Arthur Szyk, a Polish Jew who would settle in the United States and become a well-known illustrator and political artist. The East End has a long association with the Jewish community. The oldest surviving synagogue in the UK, Bevis Marks, was built here in 1701. From the late 1880s, following persecution in Eastern Europe, tens of thousands of Jews arrived in Whitechapel.

Continue along the high street. Look up at the frontage of

Further along the high street, use the traffic lights to cross into Altab Ali Park ahead ❺ The wrought-iron arch was installed in 1989 and designed by David Peterson as a fusion of Bangladeshi and English Gothic architecture. As you read earlier, the East End was a hub of Jewish immigration in the 19th century and from the mid-20th century it would become the centre of the Bengali community in London.

Altab Ali Park was once St Mary's churchyard. From the 13th century a large chapel known as St Mary Matfelon stood here, its whitewashed

stone walls giving it the nickname the 'White Chapel'. Structurally unsound by the 19th century, it was rebuilt in 1877, only to be damaged by a fire in 1880, which gutted most of the building. It was rebuilt again in 1882 but then destroyed during the Blitz and never rebuilt. The only reminders of the church are the scattered tombs in the park.

The park's name was changed in 1998 to mark the 20-year anniversary of the murder of Altab Ali, a 25-year-old Bangladeshi man who was stabbed to death during a racially motivated attack. Sadly, this incident was by no means unique, but one of several serious and fatal incidents of racist attacks in the area during the 1970s and 1980s. However, it did ignite a political response; 10 days after Ali's death, 7,000 people gathered in the park to march with his coffin to 10 Downing Street amid calls of 'black and white, unite and fight'.

Also in the park, you can find a large red-and-white monument known as the Shaheed Minar (Martyr's Monument) ❻ It is a smaller replica of the original in Dhaka, Bangladesh, which commemorates the activists killed while protesting the right to use their mother tongue of Bengali in 1952. Bengali gained official status in Pakistan alongside Urdu in 1956.

Exit the park and continue along Whitechapel Road.

Shortly on your right, on the corner of Fieldgate Street, you will see the faded yellow frontage of the former Whitechapel Bell Foundry ❼ Established in the 1570s, the foundry continuously manufactured bells here until it ceased trading in 2017. To put that in perspective, the foundry lasted from the reign of Queen Elizabeth I (r. 1558–1603) until Queen Elizabeth II (r. 1952–present). The most famous bells cast here include Big Ben and the Liberty Bell in Philadelphia.

The original 16th-century location is thought to have been around Gunthorpe Street, but the foundry moved to this site sometime around

Below Whitechapel Bell Foundry

the mid-1740s and the current building is now grade II* listed. With declining demand and the fact that bells tend to last for centuries, the building is set to be redeveloped into a boutique hotel. However, the Whitechapel Bells brand has been licensed and continues to cast bells in the UK.

Turn right, and then left, onto Fieldgate Street. Continuing on Fieldgate Street, you will pass the Maryam Centre, part of the East London Mosque, on your left. The East London Mosque Trust was established in 1910, with a view to building a mosque in East London. They purchased buildings along Commercial Street in 1940 but moved to their current location in 1985.

Shortly on your left you will reach Tower House ❽ Converted into flats between 2005 and 2008, this building was originally known as Rowton

House, Whitechapel. Rowton Houses were established in London in the 1890s to provide decent, low-cost, housing for single working men. The scheme was personally financed by Lord Rowton, philanthropist and private secretary to Benjamin Disraeli from 1866–81. As well as basic private rooms containing a bed, chair and chamber pot, Rowton Houses were equipped with washrooms, a dining room, reading rooms, a barber's shop and a boot-cleaning room. The bedrooms were inaccessible during the day to ensure all the occupants were out at work. By the 1970s the building was deemed unfit as housing and fell into dereliction.

Continue on Fieldgate Street until you reach New Road. Turn right here, and then left, onto Newark Street. Ahead you will see the somewhat extraordinary sight of what appears to be a giant hedgehog's behind ❾ Part of Queen Mary University, and officially called the Neuron Pod, it was designed by British architect Will Alsop and is used for hosting science workshops and event hire. The building is purposefully playful, designed to pique your curiosity, with the aim of encouraging more people – especially children – to visit the venue.

Cross Turner Street and, continuing along Newark Street, you

will shortly see the former church of St Augustine with St Philip ⑩ Completed in 1892 by Arthur Cawston, it is now used as a private library for medicine and dentistry students of Queen Mary University. However, the former crypt of the church is still accessible to the public as the Royal London Hospital Museum.

The London Hospital opened in Whitechapel in 1740, a small-scale building surrounded by fields and funded by philanthropists and businessmen. By the end of the 19th century it was the largest hospital in the country and at the forefront of new training and medical innovations. Elizabeth Garrett Anderson, born in Whitechapel in 1812, completed some of her training here and would go on to become the first woman to qualify as a doctor in Britain. Another woman who trained here was Edith Cavell.

During the First World War Cavell was working in German-occupied Belgium and helped 200 Allied soldiers escape. She was subsequently arrested and executed by firing squad in 1915. The museum contains a letter written by Edith Cavell to her fellow nurses a day before her death. She signs it 'I have loved you all much more than you thought'. Also in the museum you can read about the story of Joseph Merrick, known as the 'Elephant Man'

due to his severe physical deformities. He lived in the London Hospital until his death in 1890, well cared for and away from gawping members of the public.

Following the map, turn right onto Turner Street, then left onto Ashfield Street, to reach Ford Square. The older houses here are surviving white stucco terraces from the late 18th century, and this and neighbouring Sidney Square are both part of a protected conservation area. Continue on Ashfield Street and pause at no. 91 ⑪ Look up to spot a blue plaque to Sir Jack Cohen, founder of Tesco supermarket chain. Cohen was born in 1898 to a Jewish family in Whitechapel and grew up in this house, serving in the Royal Flying Corps during the First World War, before establishing a market trader's stall in Hackney. After running a number of stalls, he developed a wholesale business and, in 1924, created the Tesco brand, combining the first syllable of his surname and the initials of his business partner TE Stockwell.

Continue on Ashfield Street to turn left onto Sidney Street. Look out for the small red plaque on the side of Wexford House ⑫ This is the only visible reminder of the so-called Siege of Sidney Street. On a Friday night

Right Sidney Street plaque

in December 1910, a mile from here in Houndsditch, a botched robbery took place in a jeweller's shop. During attempts to tunnel into the shop from next door, neighbours overheard banging and the police were called. As the police arrived the robbers burst out onto the pavement, shooting three officers dead. Also killed in the fray – apparently shot in the back by an accomplice – was the gang's leader Poloski Morountzeff. The gang scattered and a joint investigation was launched by the Metropolitan and City police forces to find the others responsible. Police assembled at 100 Sidney Street in the early hours of 3 January 1911, now the site of Wexford House, where two remaining gang members were believed to be hiding.

The police surrounded the building and were met with gunshots from inside. A 36-year-old Winston Churchill (Home Secretary at the time) was also on the scene and approved the deployment of troops from the Tower of London, as well as Royal Engineers, who were ordered to blow up the house. At 1am the house caught fire and Churchill only allowed the fire brigade to enter the building once the firing from inside had stopped. In the end two bodies were discovered and found to be petty criminals. This was rather less sensational than the Eastern European anarchists that newspapers had speculated about amid a climate of anti-immigration rhetoric. The red plaque commemorates Charles Pearson, a fire officer who was struck by falling masonry on entering the building and who was paralyzed, eventually passing away six months after the siege.

Further up Sidney Street, keep an eye out for the golden statue of Sheikh Mujibur Rahman, a leader of Bangladesh's independence who became the first president (and later prime minister) of the country in 1971, but was assassinated in 1975. The location has no connection with Rahman and was an independent project of local resident Afsar Khan

Sadek who decided to commission the sculpture at his own expense, installing it in his front garden.

Continue up Sidney Street to reach the busy Mile End Road. On the opposite corner, you will see the Blind Beggar pub ⓭ And beside the pub is the yellow-brick building of a former brewery established in 1808 and now private flats ⓮ The Blind Beggar is one of the East End's more famous pubs, notorious as the site of the murder of George Cornell, shot dead by gangster Ronnie Kray in 1966. The building dates from 1894, but the name hints at a far older legend of a 13th-century nobleman (possibly Henry de Montfort), who disguised himself as a blind beggar in order to find an appropriate match for his charming daughter Bessy. When the suitors learned Bessy only had a blind beggar for a father, their love mysteriously faded, all apart from one who in his selflessness proved himself worthy and the pair lived happily ever after.

> 'All things were made ready they
> went hand in hand
> Young Billy and Betsey were both
> made as one,
> e's the most beautiful damsel that
> ever was seen,
> 's the blind beggar's daughter of
> Bethnal green.'

During a botched robbery in a jeweller's shop in Houndsditch, the robbers panicked, burst out onto the pavement and shot three police officers dead.

Cross over Mile End Road and turn right. Shortly on your left, you will see an incredible 17th-century survivor. Set back from the road are the Trinity Green Almshouses, built in 1695 as a charitable project to house retired sailors ⓯ Two exquisite sculpted boats can be seen atop pillars on either side of the entrance. The money for the project was provided by Captain Henry Mudd of Ratcliffe, who gave the land to Trinity House, a charity dedicated to supporting shipping and the seafaring community (see also, page 24).

A little further along Mile End Road, you will see a mural from 2012 by Mychael Barratt. It features the Whitechapel Gallery and Bell Foundry, as well as the Kray twins striding

menacingly through the crowd. Two figures that might come as a surprise are Mahatma Ghandi (who stayed in Bow in 1931) chatting to Bushra Nasir, who in 1993 became the first Muslim woman in the United Kingdom to become a headteacher. Looking a little like a disapproving parking warden, the man with a book in hand is William Booth, a Methodist preacher who, along with his wife Catherine, founded the Salvation Army in 1865. The couple also appear as statues on your right-hand side, both depicted preaching to crowds, which they did regularly here in the 19th century.

As you continue along the Mile End Road, you may have to look twice at the impressive building located at

numbers 69–89. Built in the 1920s, it was part of a grand plan for Wickham's department store, which aspired to build the Harrod's of the East End. The only issue was that one tenant wouldn't sell up. Look up at the smaller white facade in the middle of the larger surrounding buildings and you will see the name Spiegelhalter Bros Ltd **16** The Spiegelhalters were German immigrants who established a jeweller's and watchmaker's shop in 1828. By the early 1900s they were based on this location, next door to Wickham's department store. Having already moved location once for Wickham's they refused to do so again and so the new department store was built around them. The Spiegelhalters

Opposite Trinity Green Almshouses
Left Former Wickham's department store

the top of the auditorium, supported only by her incredibly strong jaw biting down on a piece of leather! Further along the Mile End Road, at nos 107–13, you will find a wonderful group of 18th-century houses. They were restored in the early 1990s by the Spitalfields Trust, but were first built in 1717 by Anthony Ireland.

Cross Mile End Road into Stepney Green. Keep an eye out for a curious domed metal shaft on the left, one of London's wonderfully named 'stink pipes'. Scattered across London they are linked with sewage pipes belowground and were installed to help prevent dangerous build-ups of gases, which could lead to explosions. Shortly on your right you will see a ghost sign for Daren Bread, a household brand in the early 20th century ⓲ There was a bakery here from the 19th century until the 1970s.

Follow the map to walk through Stepney Green Gardens. Within this quiet, residential enclave, the oldest house is no. 37, built in 1694. It remains a private home following restoration by the Spitalfields Trust ⓳ It was built for Dormer Sheppard, a wealthy West Indian merchant who, according to newspaper reports, owned 'a black boy named Lewis, about 15 years old'. A later owner of the property was Dame Mary Gayer, widow of an East India

had the last laugh, outliving the department store by 20 years and still going as a family business in Penzance. The larger building was recently renovated as office space and thankfully retained this historic quirk.

Next door is one of the best independent cinemas in London, the Genesis Cinema ⓱ Prior to becoming a cinema, this site had a long history of entertainment venues, starting with the Eagle Tavern from 1848 and then as various music halls including Lusby's, the Paragon and Empire. As well as the usual music and dancing, in 1877, this site hosted a performance by Madame Sanyeah, one of – if not *the* – first female aerial acrobat. Her most famous trick was to be raised to

Opposite No. 37 Stepney Green Gardens
Left (top) Stepney Green Gardens;
(bottom) Stepney Green Station

As you walk through Stepney Green Gardens, with their striking blue cobblestones, you will feel as if you have stepped back in time.

Company governor – the entwined letters of M and G can be seen on the gate. **Exit Stepney Green via Hayfield Passage to rejoin Mile End Road.**

Ahead is Anchor Retail Park, site of a huge brewery established in the 18th century by Robert Westfield who later partnered with Joseph Moss and eventually, John Charrington **20** By 1807 it was the second-largest brewery in London. You can see the remains of the offices, built in 1872, on the corner of Cephas Avenue. Continuing up Mile End Road, are surviving homes of the brewery owners. Originally these were three houses, built in 1742, but only two stand today, numbers 133–5 and 137–9 known as Malplaquet House **21**

Ahead is Stepney Green Station where the walk ends 22 The station opened in 1902, and as you go inside look out for the ghost sign pointing you down 'To The Trains'.

IN FOCUS • FIRE INSURANCE MARKS

The Great Fire of London was an unprecedented disaster. Raging for almost five days, its effects were lasting and some changes are visible today.

The City of London was accustomed to fires. Houses were closely packed together and largely built from combustible materials, while people built fires in their homes for warmth or for their work. This proved a dangerous combination.

Previously the general response to managing fires in the City was either to try and quench the flames with buckets of water or squirts (early fire hoses) or else to tear down homes to create fire breaks. In 1668 the onus was placed on local authorities to stock equipment necessary for firefighting – things like leather buckets and ladders – but this still was not a foolproof plan.

After the devastation of the Great Fire of London, which left an estimated £10 million worth of damage, a number of people spotted a business opportunity: fire insurance.

Hot off the mark was Nicholas Barbon, a property developer and economist. In 1681 he founded the Insurance Office for Houses, the world's first private insurance firm. Barbon died in 1698, paving the way for many other companies to follow.

These companies hired the first firefighters – Thames watermen – who were paid for their services. In an early marketing ploy, companies would try to make their watermen look the best, creating special, easily recognizable uniforms.

The first fire marks

The Sun Fire Office went one step further. In 1706 Charles Povey, who had witnessed the Great Fire's destruction, became determined to help others protect their livelihoods and possessions. In 1710 the Sun Fire Office was established, which had the idea of placing a mark on the walls of properties, distinguishing their customers and identifying their policy numbers under their symbol. The first 'fire mark' had been created and the company still exists today, as the Royal Sun Alliance (RSA). Fire marks were quickly adopted by other companies and you can spot them across London, and the United Kingdom, today.

The different marks have given rise to a theory that perhaps rival companies wouldn't put out fires on

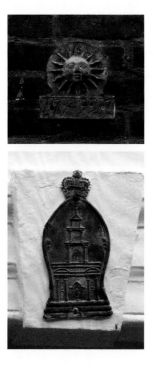

Top Sun Fire Office fire mark;
Bottom Royal Exchange
Assurance fire mark

buildings that were not their responsibility. In reality early firefighters were encouraged to put out any fire they came across, regardless of the owner's insurance status, which is certainly a bit more heartwarming!

Fire marks to spot

The Royal Exchange Assurance was established in 1720, offering insurance against a variety of situations and specializing in protecting ships and merchandise at sea. Its fire mark takes the form of the Royal Exchange (see page 32), where its offices were based. In 1968 the Royal Exchange Assurance merged with Guardian Assurance, founded in 1821, whose mark shows the goddess Athena striding through clouds with an olive branch in one hand and a spear in the other.

The Hand-in-Hand Fire and Life Insurance company was founded in 1696, lasting until 1905 when it was transferred into Commerical Union. It is now part of Aviva.

The Phoenix Fire Office was founded in 1680, using the apt symbol of a mythical bird rising amid flames.

The Fire Watch
Between St Paul's Cathedral and Millennium Bridge stands this memorial to the Fire Watch, a voluntary organization that protected the cathedral from bombing raids during the First and Second World Wars. Although they received training, these weren't professional firefighters, but rather drawn from professions as varied as architects, civil servants and members of the clergy.

An organized fire service
In 1833 the London Fire Engine Establishment (LFEE) was formed by the merging of 10 different insurance company teams. Throughout the 18th and early 19th centuries London had grown tremendously, and alongside this was the growing number of industrial trades that were fire hazards,

not to mention the crowded riverside wharves that stored oil, alcohol, cotton and other highly flammable goods.

In 1861 tragedy struck in the Great Fire of Tooley Street. Packed warehouses saw explosions and flames that tore through connected wharves at an alarming rate. It took two weeks to fully extinguish the fire and the resulting costs were around £166 million in today's money. It also claimed the lives of six people, among them the superintendent of the LFEE, James Braidwood. A memorial to him, and the fire, can be seen on Tooley Street today.

With the growing costs of insuring and extinguishing fires, private companies no longer wanted to shoulder the responsibility and, in 1865, the Metropolitan Fire Brigade Act was passed, establishing a public service and the modern fire brigade.

Opposite (top) Hand-in-Hand Fire and Life Insurance fire mark; **(bottom)** Phoenix Fire Office fire mark
Above Tooley Street memorial

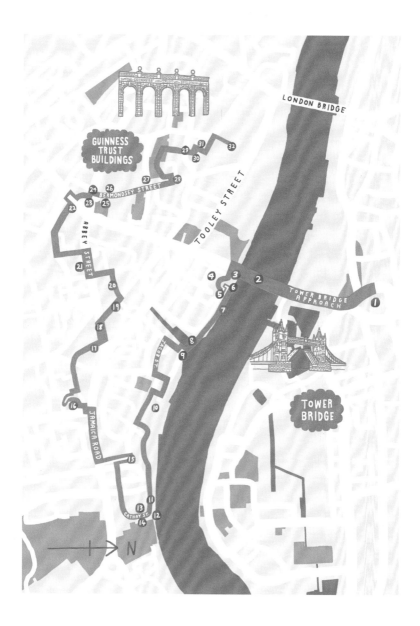

Shad Thames and Bermondsey walk

START
Tower Gateway Station (DLR)

FINISH
London Bridge Station

DISTANCE
5.7km (3.5 miles)

The name 'Bermondsey' comes from the Saxon lord, Beormund, who owned this marshy island (*ea* or *ey*) centuries ago. The geography and proximity to the river have heavily influenced this area and you will see historic links throughout the walk.

However, the most striking visual themes are remnants of the once-mighty industrial hubs, former warehouses, factories and engineering projects that changed the landscape of London forever. As the working-class population boomed, so too did the need for social and welfare services. Bermondsey bred a number of inspiring individuals and philanthropic organizations who worked tirelessly to improve the living standards for south-east Londoners.

Opposite View of Tower Bridge from
Bermondsey Wall East

The walk starts at Tower Gateway
Station on Docklands Light Railway
(DLR), which opened in 1987 ❶ This
was the original Central London
terminus for the DLR, connecting the
new development in the Docklands
and Canary Wharf with the City of
London. Before the purpose-built
London Docks arrived (around 1800),
river trade was concentrated in the
Pool of London, the area between
London Bridge and Tower Bridge.
On the walk today you will see many
reminders of this industrial past.

**Cross Tower Hill, making your
way towards Tower Bridge.** Shortly
on your right you will pass the Tower
of London. Built in the 1080s and
enlarged by successive monarchs, it
has served as a royal palace, a fortress
and a prison. The outer walls, seen on
the approach to Tower Bridge, were
finished around 1300. When it was
decided to build another river crossing
south of London Bridge, Parliament
wanted the design of the bridge to
reflect the medieval appearance of
the Tower of London. So the bridge,
while it seems old-looking, is relatively
recent, completed in 1894 and
designed by Sir Horace Jones, with
John Wolfe Barry as engineer.

The second stipulation in the
design was that it needed to allow tall
ships to move freely beneath it, so a

*Today the Tower
of London
is one of the
capital's most
visited tourist
attractions,
thanks largely to
the crown jewels.*

minimum width of 61m (200ft) and
42m (135ft) headroom were required.
The result is a technologically
advanced bridge that opens in the
middle, disguised as a medieval Gothic
relic. Horace Jones described it as
'steel skeletons clothed in stone'.

Another sneaky element can be
spotted on the north side of the
bridge. Look closely at the row of blue
lampposts, and you will see that one
stands out from the others as missing
its lamp. This is because it was once
a cast-iron chimney, connected to
a coal fire in a guard room, keeping
the soldiers on duty warm. After the
passing of the Clean Air Act of 1956,
coal fires were banned in Central
London, but this survives as a quirky
reminder hiding in plain sight.

Left (top) Guard-room chimney on Tower Bridge; **(bottom)** Cock's foot in Courage Yard

Walk over Tower Bridge, taking in the views over Central London on your right and Canary Wharf on your left ❷ Make sure you look down at the centre of the bridge to spot the gap where the piers open, and look up to see the glass floors of the Tower Bridge walkways that can be visited and – if you're feeling brave – walked across. Amid the decoration of the bridge, you might also spot a curious symbol of a circle and 'x' surmounted by a cross. This is the Bridge Mark, emblem of the City Bridge Trust, whose history dates back to 1282 when a charity, Bridge House Estates, was given a royal charter to maintain London Bridge. This fund survives today, managing the bridges within the City of London and – among other charitable work – it paid for the construction of Blackfriars Bridge and the ongoing maintenance of the Millennium Bridge.

As you approach the south side of the bridge, look out for the renovated flats on the left-hand side. Until 1981 this was the Anchor Brewhouse, a brewery first established by John Courage in 1787.

Descend the steps and walk under the bridge to reach Shad Thames. From here you get a spectacular view back towards Tower Bridge. If the gate is open and it's low tide you may

Left (top) Shad Thames; **(bottom)** view of the City Thames Path

also want to follow the map down Horsleydown Old Stairs onto the foreshore for a more impressive view ❸ **Returning to Shad Thames, cross into Courage Yard ❹** It is named after John Courage, who established the brewery here. The symbol of Courage Ales was a fighting cock and if you look down within the development you can see metal cockerels' feet embedded into the pavement.

Return to Shad Thames ❺ This area was once known as the Larder of London, where spices, tea and coffee were imported until the 1970s and surviving wrought-iron bridges are a reminder of a frenetic industrial scene of loading, hauling and moving goods.

Since the 1980s this area has been transformed with residential developments and a smattering of commercial units and restaurants. **Backtrack slightly to walk towards the riverfront along a street called Maggie Blake's Cause ❻** This is named after a local activist who, in the 1990s, campaigned to save the riverfront views as a public right of way, so it's thanks to Maggie that we can enjoy the views back towards Central London. **Continue along Thames Path and you will soon pass Butler's Wharf on your right ❼** These converted warehouses were first built 1871–3 and are grade II listed.

a squalid tangle of slum housing and warehouses that teetered over the dirty water channels. The journalist Henry Mayhew, writing in 1849, calls it 'pest island' and says 'the air has literally the smell of a graveyard'. It was demolished and covered over following a cholera outbreak of 1850. Today an altogether more pleasant living environment can be seen in the Downings Road Moorings **9** This collection of historic trading barges, lighters and tugboats provides affordable homes and studios for a community of around 70 people.

Follow Thames Path through China Wharf and continue along Bermondsey Wall West. Pause at the riverfront to admire the view back towards Central London, then follow Thames Path to rejoin the riverfront at Bermondsey Wall East. This route skirts around Chambers Wharf, home to one of the main drive sites of London's 'super sewer', Tideway **10** In 2020 the Tunnel Boring Machine, 'Selina', started her journey 5.5km (3½ miles) under London and the River Thames towards Abbey Mills in Stratford. Selina takes her name from Selina Fox, a doctor working in Bermondsey during the late 19th and early 20th centuries, who founded Bermondsey Medical Mission in 1904, treating thousands of poor, local

After a short walk you reach St Saviour's Dock, originally the mouth of the River Neckinger. St Saviour's takes its name from a mill run by the monks of Bermondsey Abbey until 1541, when it passed into secular hands during the Reformation. As for Neckinger, it is thought that the name derives from 'neckercher' as in a neckerchief worn around the neck. This could be a reference to the looping path of the river, or to the more gruesome tradition of hanging pirates at this dock to act as a deterrent to would-be thieves.

Cross the footbridge (constructed in 1995) 8 Be thankful you are not walking this path in the 19th century. The area was known as Jacob's Island,

residents who would otherwise have been without healthcare. She was awarded an MBE in 1938.

Whenever there's construction work under London there's the opportunity for new archaeological discoveries and the Chambers Wharf site did not disappoint. Back in 2018, the Museum of London Archaeology (MOLA) team made a startling discovery of a male skeleton lying face-down in the mud, his preserved leather boots still clearly visible. The boots were dated to the late 15th or early 16th century and from the examination of his body, the MOLA team suspect he made his living working by the river 500 years ago, his skeleton showing signs of osteoarthritis despite being under the age of 35. It serves as a reminder of the back-breaking physical labour and the ever-present danger of working alongside the River Thames.

Continue along Bermondsey Wall East until you reach an unusual collection of sculptures ⓫ This artwork is called *Dr Salter's Daydream*, by Diane Gorvin, and was first unveiled in 1991. A bespectacled man with a hat and umbrella half waves to a little girl with her back to the wall. The man is Dr Alfred Salter, who, after studying medicine at Guy's Hospital, came to work in Bermondsey and was shocked

by the poverty he saw. He opened a medical practice to help working-class residents, offering free services when people couldn't afford them. In 1900 he married Ada, also depicted here, and they strived to improve the lives of Bermondsey residents. Alfred was elected to Bermondsey Borough Council and later became an MP while Ada was appointed Mayor of Bermondsey in 1922, London's first female mayor.

The couple paid the ultimate sacrifice for their commitment to the area because their daughter Joyce caught scarlet fever and died, aged eight. In 2011 the statue of Dr Salter was stolen and the culprit never caught. Thankfully, in 2014, the sculpture was restored along with the additional figure of Ada.

Ahead is The Angel pub, grade II listed and built in the 1830s ⓬ Its riverside rooms offer a great place to

stop for a drink or food and admire the views. **Leaving the pub, walk down Cathay Street.** On your right is a Scheduled Monument – an important archaeological site. Here are the remains of a moated manor house built 1349–56 as a residence of King Edward III (r. 1327–77) **⓭** It would once have been a grand building complete with hall, kitchen and chapel, but after Edward's death in 1377 it fell into the hands of Bermondsey Abbey.

To your left on Cathay Street is the council-owned Cathay House **⓮** Above a central door you can spot the red and blue shield of the Metropolitan Borough of Bermondsey, the local authority between 1900 and 1965. Part of the crest shows a lion with a crozier (bishop's staff) and a 'B' either side, which is derived from the insignia of Bermondsey Abbey.

At the crossroads ahead, turn right onto Paradise Street, walking past the 1950s' Pynfold Estate, social housing constructed by the Metropolitan Borough of Bermondsey. At West Lane, cross the road to continue through Dixons Alley until you reach Wilson Grove. Turn right, towards Emba Street. Here, you can stop to admire the cottage-like housing that was built in 1928 and designed by Culpin & Bowers as a remedy to the slum clearance of

the area **⓯** These houses are about as far away from the overcrowded housing of Jacob's Island than could possibly be imagined and were an embodiment of the healthy and wholesome living conditions that the Salters had envisaged for all Bermondsey residents.

Retrace your steps on Wilson Grove and continue until you reach the busy Jamaica Road, then turn right. The road takes its name from Jamaica House, which stood on Cherry Garden Street from the early 1600s until around 1860. It is mentioned by Pepys who visited in 1667 and describes a rural day out where his maids ran across the bowling green.

Walk along Jamaica Road, past Bermondsey Station. This Jubilee line station opened in 1999 and stands on the site of Alfred Salter's surgery. **Cross Jamaica Road to walk down St James's Road, passing the mock-Tudor Gregorian pub.** It was rebuilt after the Second World War but there's been a pub here since at least 1822. **Step into St James's Churchyard ⓰** St James's Church was built with funds following the victory at the Battle of Waterloo, so is known as one of the 'Waterloo' or 'Commissioners' churches and was completed in 1829, designed by James Savage. Its size and grandeur hint at a

Left (top) Granite 'slide' at St James's Church; **(bottom)** 22nd Battalion war memorial

community that was rapidly growing – indeed Bermondsey had risen from under 10,000 people in the 1720s to almost 60,000 in the 1820s and peaked at around 130,000 in 1900.

As such, the largely poor and working-class community was lacking in green and open spaces, especially for children. In 1921 Arthur Carr, chairman of the Peek Freans biscuit factory, noticed some local children playing on the steps of St James's, using a sloping granite slab as a makeshift slide. Later that year he gifted a new, impressive playground for the children of Bermondsey featuring what became known as the Joy Slide. Sadly, by the 1980s it had been vandalized and was in a sorry state. However, exactly 100 years after the original was erected, Arthur's great-great-grandson designed a new slide to delight the children of Bermondsey once again! You can find the new Joy Slide on the south side of the church.

Leave the churchyard, taking a left onto Old Jamaica Road. Shortly on your left, set within a block of contemporary flats you'll see a First World War memorial to the 22nd Battalion, the London Regiment, whose drill hall once stood on the same street **17 Turn left onto Abbey Street.** Ahead you will see the viaduct,

with trains running into London Bridge Station. It was constructed between 1834 and 1836 and contains almost 900 arches, leap-frogging over buildings to Deptford Creek. It carried the first passenger railway in London and is grade II listed.

Before turning right onto Druid Street, look up to your left, to admire the facade of the Neckinger Mills 🔞 Built around 1864, it housed the warehouses for Bevington and Sons, one of the biggest tanneries in 19th-century Bermondsey, noted for producing fine, soft leather. Bevington and Sons leased the site from 1806, but 100 years previously, this was a paper mill run by Matthias Koops and Elias Carpenter, who produced recycled paper made from straw and wood. Both industrial ventures relied on the River Neckinger seen earlier on the walk, the tidal flow of which provided fresh water daily.

Follow the viaduct along Druid Street and a theme emerges. The arches are home to multiple brewery bars and bottle shops, part of what is unofficially known as the Bermondsey Beer Mile 🔞 The renovation and gentrification of these viaducts is part of The Low Line, which manages 'hubs' in Flat Iron Square, Borough Market and – found just up ahead – Maltby Street Market. **Turn left**

onto Milstream Road, passing under the viaduct and with Maltby Street Market on your right 🔞 It opened in 2010 and has now become a kind of cooler younger brother to Borough Market. At the weekend the street fills with food stalls, alongside the more established restaurants, cafes and bars nestled in the arches.

At the end of Milstream Road turn left on Maltby Street then right onto Abbey Street. During the Second World War Bermondsey's large number of factories and proximity to the docks in Rotherhithe made it a target for the Luftwaffe. At nos 122–32 Abbey Street you can see a surviving chunk of early-19th-century housing where its neighbours were obliterated

far more rural reference. It serves as a reminder that this was once a path where the monks would walk from the abbey buildings and into their farmland or 'grange'.

After crossing Fendell Street, on your left you will see Grange Walk Mews, once part of the 19th-century infants' school as the stone plaque recalls and renovated into housing in the 1980s. On the other side of the street is no. 67 Grange Walk. Built in the early 18th century, this has all the appearance of a home for an up-and-coming merchant or businessman. Today it is still a private home and is grade II listed. Peer around the corner to admire the ghost sign on its side wall. The faded letters of 'E Spaull & Co' are a reminder of Elizabeth Spaull, a clay pipe manufacturer from Norfolk who moved to London after her marriage and ran the business under her own name when her husband Henry died in 1873. Elizabeth died in 1923 but the firm continued operating from this address until 1943, making clay pipes, chinaware and matches.

by bombs **21** **Continue along Abbey Street and then turn left into The Grange.** It may not seem that way, but you are approaching the historic centre of Bermondsey, the abbey founded in the 11th century. You are now walking through St Saviour's Estate, built in the 1960s, where each block has a link with the abbey: Rufus, after King William Rufus who granted the French monks further land around 1090, and the names of abbots Attilburgh, Tomson and Bromleigh. **Turn right into Grange Walk.** This street is an eclectic mix of historic and post-Second World War buildings, making it visually clear where the bombs fell during the Blitz. The name – as you may have guessed – has a

Return to the south side of the street and head to the corner with Grigg's Place. Here you can see another historic educational link, as this was the Bermondsey United Charity School for Girls, now converted into flats. The building

Left Bermondsey Square

2014, but back in 1902 it was a shiny new public convenience, one of 23 across the Borough of Southwark, all of which are now closed. Another clue to something brewing underground is the towering cast-iron green stink pipe nearby, which acts as a vent for unpleasant gases, releasing them high above the heads (and nostrils) of passersby.

Cross over Tower Bridge Road, cutting through to Bermondsey Square ㉓ This is the site of the weekly antiques market and – further back in time – Bermondsey Abbey. Although there was an earlier religious settlement here, Bermondsey Abbey is first mentioned in the Domesday Book as founded in 1082 by Aylwin Childe. It was dedicated to St Saviour (literally meaning Holy Saviour, or Jesus) and grew to be one of the most important and wealthiest monastic organizations in England. When it was dissolved by King Henry VIII (r. 1509–47) the buildings and land were divided up and replaced with grand houses, occupied by high-ranking noblemen and courtiers during the 16th century.

Today it's hard to get a sense of how impressive a complex the abbey would have been, but between 1984 and 1995 an extensive archaeological dig by MOLA revealed a large church

dates from 1830 but the organization is older, founded in 1712 for boys and expanding to include girls a decade later. In total they took the responsibility for educating 220 boys and 130 girls.

Continue along Grange Walk until you reach no. 11 ㉒ This higgledy-piggledy collection of houses, running until no. 5 at the end, was built in the late 17th century, and within nos 5–7 is the medieval abbey gatehouse. Make sure you look up to spot the fire mark (see also, pages 130–3) above no. 9.

Turn left onto Tower Bridge Road. Ahead is a triangular traffic island with a structure surrounded by black railings. Today this is Bermondsey Arts Club, a cocktail bar that opened in

Right The Old Rectory

as well as a cloister, kitchens and a hall. A further redevelopment project in 2004 for Bermondsey Square resulted in the new apartment buildings, hotel and retail space along the ground floor. But there is a way to see the abbey ruins today. Head into the Turkish Restaurant, Lokma, at 11 Bermondsey Square and below the glass floors of its cocktail bar you can see the medieval stones of the abbey.

Exit Bermondsey Square onto Bermondsey Street. As you cross Abbey Street take note of the small white building, now the coffee shop WatchHouse **24** This used to be a real 19th-century watch house, where guards would keep a lookout over the graveyard for potential body snatchers – so-called 'resurrection men' who would steal freshly buried corpses and then sell them for medical research.

Continue on Bermondsey Street. Shortly on your right is the stuccoed, Gothic facade of St Mary Magdalene **25** This was the medieval parish church of Bermondsey that catered for the whole of the area until St James's Church (seen earlier) was built. Although some of the internal fabric and parts of the tower may date to the 15th century, the rest was rebuilt 1675–99. Next to the church is no. 191, The Old Rectory, a charming early-19th-century house that has

the Bermondsey Abbey lion insignia beside the door.

Before continuing along Bermondsey Street make sure you look up to admire the flowery writing that proclaims 'Time and Talents Settlement' were based in this building dating from 1907 **26** The charity was founded in 1887 on the premise that upper-middle-class young women could better themselves by dedicating their time and talents to the less fortunate women of Bermondsey, teaching them useful skills such as singing, needlework and basket-making. It is heartening to know that the charity still exists in Rotherhithe today, serving the local community by leading social events and a

Left (top) Times and Talents Settlement building; **(bottom)** *The Shared*, by Austin Emery

variety of workshops from practising mindfulness to playing the ukulele.

Continue along Bermondsey Street, the ancient high street that connected the abbey with the River Thames. The street has a creative feel thanks to the colourful Fashion and Textile Museum (founded in 2003 by Dame Zandra Rhodes) and White Cube gallery, which opened in 2011. There's also a good selection of (mostly) independent restaurants, cafes and shops, so it is hard to believe that until relatively recently this whole area would have absolutely stunk.

This was the centre of the leather industry from the 18th century, the tidal surges from the Neckinger powering the machinery while pits of urine and excrement were kept nearby for curing hides. Charles Dickens Junior in his *Dictionary of London* (1879) summarizes the scene: 'the air reeks with evil smells . . . The warehouse round are all full of tanned hides; the yards behind the high walls are all tanneries, with their tens of thousands of hides soaking in the pits'.

Reminders of this trade abound, from the obvious Leathermarket and Tanner Streets to the subtler Morocco Store, emblazoned across a late-19th-century warehouse building, now flats ❷ This is a reference to the highly prized goat skin that resulted in fine

Left (top) Horseshoe Inn; **(bottom)**
Melior Street Community Garden

leather that was used for gloves, shoes and book-binding.

While on Bermondsey Street, stop to admire no. 78, which dates from the late 17th century with a wonderful oriel window, jettying out over the ground floor, and topped with a colourful, weatherboarded attic space. Now rare, this type of building was once commonplace across London and would have been home to ordinary, working Londoners.

Another architectural treat can be found in the curved shopfronts of nos 68–70 **28** Dating from the mid-18th century, again, today they seem extraordinary because of their scarcity, but they were the homes of regular people. One resident of no. 70 was Henry Clemson. He married his second wife Jane at St Mary Magdalene in 1792 and was a coal merchant. He also seems to have contributed to the local community, taking the role of Deputy Secretary and Collector for the Asylum for the support and education of the deaf and dumb children of the poor.

Walk through the carriage arch into Carmarthen Place. Look up to admire the coade stone bearded face above you. Ahead of you is another curious stone, this time a public sculpture by Austin Emery called *The Shared*. Unveiled in 2014, it is a collective effort from the artist and assorted Bermondsey residents who took part in workshops from 2012. For another artistic endeavour, look to your right. Behind the industrial, concertina door is London Glassblowing, founded by Peter Layton in 1976, where visitors can watch the artists in action, moulding molten glass, or simply peruse the gallery space.

Follow the map through **Tyers Estate and walk through Leathermarket Gardens.** This large green space was once the site of tanneries and a glue manufacturer, but after the surrounding housing was obliterated during the Blitz, it was laid out as gardens from the 1950s. **Leave the gardens via Kirby Grove.** On your left is the attractive Guinness Trust housing estate, built in 1897 and one of eight similar projects across London **29** The trust was set up by Sir Edward Cecil Guinness, great grandson of the Guinness Brewery founder, who gave the equivalent of £25 million today to provide decent homes for ordinary people. The trust currently houses 120,000 people across England.

Continue along Kirby Grove and cross Snowsfields to enter Melior Place. You will walk past the pretty Horseshoe Inn pub, rebuilt in 1897 **30** **Turn left and then right to find**

Coade was an artificial stone, officially a ceramic, made from a recipe perfected by Eleanor Coade who ran a factory in Lambeth.

yourself in Melior Street Community Garden 31 Towering above it is the Shard, the tallest building in Western Europe. Renovated in 2007 by the London Bridge Business Improvement District, the garden has a seating area and a vegetable garden maintained by St Mungo's 'Putting Down Roots' project, which provides salad, garlic and beans to local restaurants. From this quiet corner, follow the map along Fenning Street to reach a section of a 19th-century brick viaduct and London Bridge Station, where the walk ends **32**

TOP 10 · INDEPENDENT CAFES

*Here are 10 of London's best independent cafes.
Some are historic, but others are simply wonderful places
to spend a few hours, relaxing and recuperating.*

1. Maison Bertaux, W1
This is the oldest patisserie in London, having been founded more than 150 years ago, in 1871. Pop in for a selection of delicious, freshly baked cakes, tarts and treats and head upstairs to enjoy the tiny gallery space.

2. Rinkoffs, E1
A family business since 1911, Rinkoffs has two East End locations, staying close to its roots after Hyman Rinkoff, a Ukrainian refugee, first established a bakery here. Not to be missed is the cafe's famous crodough, a tasty combination of a croissant and a doughnut.

3. Host, EC4
Set within the spectacular 17th-century church of St Mary Aldermary in the City of London, Host serves up great coffee and a wide range of treats. Sit back and gaze up at the establishment's extraordinary fan-vaulted ceiling.

4. Attendant, W1
On the face of it, drinking coffee in a former urinal might not sound the most pleasant of experiences, but this converted 1890s' public toilet is in fact a wonderful little place to escape to in the heart of Central London.

5. Prufrock, EC1
Established on Leather Lane in 2011, Prufrock serves excellent coffee and fresh food, all in a light, airy and convivial setting.

6. Townhouse, E1
Cafes really do not get more atmospheric than this wonderfully cosy basement in Spitalfields. Be sure to browse the charming selection of books and antiques on the ground floor and pay a visit to the gallery space in the cafe's garden.

7. Briki, EC1
This is a favourite spot for brunch on Exmouth Market. Stop by to enjoy a strong coffee alongside a freshly baked carrot cake.

8. V&A Cafe, SW7
The world's first museum cafe, this is almost an artwork in itself and an embodiment of the V&A's original aim to give people an extra reason to come to West London to enjoy some culture.

9. Monocle, W1
This tiny but perfectly formed Central London cafe serves up tasty lunches and great coffee. It is a busy little place, but if you do manage to grab a seat, you can enjoy a sitting-room atmosphere in which to relax for an hour or two.

10. Rosslyn, EC4
This is the place to come to for the very best coffee in the City of London. Rosslyn was established in 2018, with its founders aiming to combine an Australian cafe with the warmth of an Irish pub.

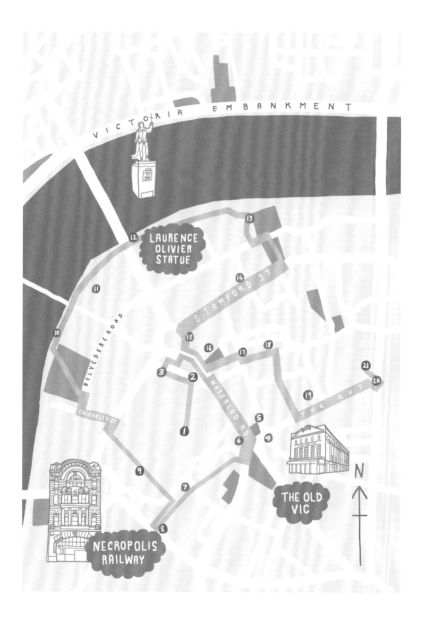

Waterloo and Southbank walk

START
Waterloo Station

FINISH
Southwark London
Underground Station

DISTANCE
1.1km (0.7 miles)

The Southbank, despite being one of the most popular destinations in London, was only developed as such after the Second World War. The Festival of Britain in 1951 took this largely industrial, working-class area and completely reinvented it, the results of which are still evident today.

The stretch of Thames Path between the London Eye and Oxo Tower is one of London's best-trodden walking routes, but this walk also ventures along the backstreets of Waterloo, tracing the area's historic nooks prior to redevelopment and telling the story of recent activists who have fought to keep their communities intact.

Right (top) Lionel Stanhope street art;
(bottom) Charles Whiffen sculpture,
Waterloo Station Opposite London
School of Mosaics panel

The walk starts from the London
Waterloo Concourse, underneath the
large four-sided clock made by Gents'
of Leicester in the 1920s ❶ You don't
need a ticket to access this area.

London Waterloo opened in 1848,
designed by William Tite, and was
enlarged in the 1920s. Built by the
London and South Western Railway
Company, it wasn't intended to be
a terminus station, but rather to
link to another station in the City of
London. Properties for the second
station were purchased, but a minor
financial crash scuppered plans.
The Waterloo & City line was built
in 1898, connecting Waterloo with
Bank (at the time named City Station)
and the line became part of London
Underground in 1994.

Leave the station via exit 3, onto
Cab Road. Ahead of you is a piece
of street art by Lionel Stanhope,
creating a faux-aged Waterloo sign
❷ One of the 'O's is replaced with
the Gents' clockface and if you look
at the time it reads 6:48pm. In the
24-hour clock, 6:48pm is, of course,
18:48, a nod to the year the station
first opened.

Turn left onto Cab Road and
walk on until you reach the main
entrance to London Waterloo
on your left ❸ This is, in fact, a
magnificent stone Victory Arch, a

memorial to the 585 London and
South Western Railway staff that died
during the First World War. Look
up at the two groups of sculptures
designed by Charles Whiffen. To
the left is 1914 and the terrifying
goddess of war, shown surrounded
by figures with hollowed-out faces,
bereft women and a startled mother
clutching a child. To the right, 1918,
is the more calming Peace. She is
framed with ears of corn, the harvest
has returned and two men and
women, although gazing thoughtfully

into the distance, look healthier as a baby contentedly sleeps, blissfully unaware of the tumultuous events of the previous years. You will revisit this post-war ambition and enthusiasm as a theme on this walk.

Cross the road here, to enter the tunnel under the railway viaduct on Mepham Street. Although sometimes covered in graffiti, through this tunnel are some attractive panels by the London School of Mosaic (formerly Southbank Mosaics, founded by David Tootill in 2004). You will see further examples of their work throughout the walk. **Turn right onto Tenison Way.** Ahead is St John's Church, built in the 1820s. It is one of the 'Waterloo churches'

named after an 1818 act of Parliament that granted up to £1 million for the building of new churches across the metropolis. The funding for this initiative followed the victory of the Napoleonic Wars, the final decisive battle of Waterloo in 1815 giving its name to both the churches built in its honour and the bridge and station seen on the walk.

Tenison Way merges with Waterloo Road. Continue until you reach the Old Vic Theatre ❹ Established in 1818, it was first named The Royal Coburg Theatre after its patron, Prince Leopold of Saxe-Coburg, who was married to Princess Charlotte, the daughter of King George IV (r. 1820–30).

Right Memorial to David Squires

Tragically, Charlotte died aged just 21 in 1817, before the Coburg opened. Following his wife's death Leopold left England in 1831 to become king of Belgium, so the theatre was on the lookout for a new patron. In 1833 the Duchess of Kent, Princess Victoria of Saxe-Coburg-Saalfeld, and the mother of the future Queen Victoria (r. 1837–1901), became the patron, so it is named after her, rather than her daughter. 'The Old Vic' was first used as the venue's name in 1871.

The gardens opposite (admittedly in need of a bit of care and attention) are named after Emma Cons, theatre manager at the Old Vic from 1880–99, who saved the theatre from financial ruin and rebranded it as an alcohol-free music hall ❺ An artist and philanthropist, Cons worked to give working-class Londoners better prospects, founding the South London Dwellings Company to provide good-quality housing, and the Coffee Music Hall Company to promote the coffee tavern as an alternative to pubs and gin palaces. The Royal Victoria Coffee Music Hall opened at the Old Vic in 1880 as part of this initiative.

Turn right onto Baylis Road. This is named after Lilian Baylis. The niece of Emma Cons, Baylis took over the running of the Old Vic in

1899. She transformed it into the renowned theatre it is today and also worked to renovate Sadler's Wells in the 1930s (see page 111). Ahead on the right is the former public library, now the Waterloo Action Centre. Take a moment to admire the mosaic of David Squires (1949–2009), the 'much-loved street sweeper' set into a brick pillar here ❻

Follow the map onto Lower Marsh. As the name suggests, the area was once rural and marshy. The street is first mentioned in 1332 as Lambeth Marsh and in the 1746 John Rocque map of London it is shown surrounded by fields and market gardens. However, by the late 1800s a popular street market flourished here, selling a mix of fresh groceries, everyday household items and other miscellaneous goods. Today you can find an assortment of street food vendors and craft stalls pitched in the street as well as a mix of shops and restaurants ❼ Look up above the corner of Leake Street and Lower Marsh and you will notice two large pots surmounted in the brickwork. These usually signify a former general store, and that oil was for sale.

The walk will continue along Leake Street, but for now take a slight detour to the end of Lower Marsh for a view to the left along Westminster Bridge Road. At no. 121 is the imposing facade of the former Necropolis Railway, London's train for the dead ❽ By the mid-1800s London's population was expanding rapidly and the small church burial grounds within the city were struggling to cope. In 1852 an ingenious – if morbid – idea was hatched by the London Necropolis Company, to transport London's dead around 40km (25 miles) out of London into Surrey, reaching their final destination at Brookwood Cemetery. The first Necropolis Station was built closer to Waterloo Station, near Leake Street today, but the Westminster Bridge Road frontage, erected in 1902 following

You can find an assortment of street food vendors and craft stalls pitched in the street at Lower Marsh.

the expansion of Waterloo Station, is the only building that survives. The Necropolis Railway ran until the early 1940s, at its peak transporting 2,000 bodies a year (as well as accompanying mourners). You could pay for different class tickets and carriages were separated according to religious denomination.

Retrace your steps along Lower Marsh and turn left down the underpass into Leake Street tunnel, the original site of the Necropolis Railway terminus. Today these tunnels, largely abandoned when the Eurostar terminal relocated to St Pancras Station, are home to The Vaults, an eclectic venue specializing in immersive theatre and alternative

Opposite Necropolis Railway building
Right Leake Street tunnel

performances. Leake Street, in particular, is also famous as a space that actively encourages street art. This tradition began in 2008 when internationally renowned street artist Banksy held an interactive exhibition, The Cans Festival, inviting artists to decorate the walls of the tunnel over the course of a weekend. The tunnel passes directly beneath all of the platforms at Waterloo Station ❾

As you emerge from Leake Street, look back to admire the former International Terminal of Waterloo Station with its blue tubular steel arched roof, designed by Nicholas Grimshaw in 1994. Grimshaw himself describes it as being 'like a great machine which sat [down] and then sort of nestled into the ground'.

Cross York Road and turn left into Chicheley Street. Ahead of you is a great view of another ambitious construction project, the London Eye. Unveiled to celebrate the millennium, the 135m (443ft) tall observation wheel is the largest of its kind in Europe and was originally intended to be temporary. However, in 2006 a new 25-year lease was agreed with the Southbank Centre, which owns the land. **Follow the map into Jubilee Gardens.** Stop here to read a little of the background to the development of this area.

In May 1951, six years after the Second World War had ended and 100 years after the famous Great Exhibition held in Hyde Park, the Festival of Britain opened. The official festival booklet described the event as 'a tonic to the nation' intended as a huge spectacle across a country that was still facing austerity and rationing, reeling from war. The aim was to showcase the best in British manufacturing and design as well as to educate and entertain visitors. Although most of the festival was temporary, a lasting effect was the introduction of a new design aesthetic, modernism, which influenced architecture, graphic design, furniture, textiles and urban

Below South Bank book market
Opposite Bernie Spain Gardens

planning. One of the major hubs of the festival was London's South Bank, kickstarting the regeneration of this area with more than 8.5 million people visiting this site across a five-month period. So, what were the major attractions?

Walk through the gardens towards the riverfront. Beside the carousel you will see a towering wooden flagpole. This was given to the festival by the Forest Industry of British Columbia and then restored as a permanent feature in 1977 to celebrate the Queen's Silver Jubilee.

Close to the flagpole, look out for a circular plaque on the floor ❿ This marks the site of the Skylon, one of the most extraordinary temporary artworks ever displayed in London. Standing at 91m (300ft), the bulk of the structure resembled a thin cigar, with points at either end. It was suspended in the air by almost invisible cables, which made it seem to float, UFO-like, on the skyline. That, coupled with it being illuminated at night, must have been an exhilarating sight. Sadly, after the festival had ended, the expense of dismantling and rebuilding the Skylon proved too costly. The prime minister at the time, Winston Churchill (who was never much of a fan), ordered it to be sold for scrap.

Continue east along the Thames Path to pass under Hungerford Bridge. It is named after Hungerford Market, which once stood on the north bank of the river. Although today the bridge carries trains into Charing Cross Station, it was first built as a suspension footbridge, which opened in 1845 and was designed by Isambard Kingdom Brunel. In 1859 South Eastern Railway bought the bridge and had it extensively remodelled to accommodate trains. Early footways added either side were never satisfactory and today the rail bridge is flanked by the far wider and safer Golden Jubilee Bridges, completed in 2002.

As you emerge from under the bridge, to your right is the only building that survives from the main festival site, The Royal Festival Hall ⓫ Today this is a performance venue

Left The Oxo Tower
Opposite Gabriel's Wharf

as a cultural destination for decades to come. The structure is brutalist in design, from the French *beton brut* meaning 'raw concrete'. At the base of the building is the graffiti-clad skatepark, regarded as the birthplace of British skateboarding where, from the early 1970s, skateboarders started using the undercroft, finding the architectural features perfect for practising tricks.

Follow the map to pass under Waterloo Bridge. Here, you will find a book market, open daily, and selling second-hand books, print and comics. After Waterloo Bridge is another large, brutalist building, the National Theatre. The theatre spent its first 13 years (1963–76) in the Old Vic, before moving to its South Bank home. The building was designed by Sir Denys Lasdun and completed in 1976. He had never designed a performance space before and, in stark contrast to other architectural firms who arrived in partners and groups, Lasdun presented a solo pitch for the prestigious commission. The first artistic director, Laurence Olivier, described this pluckiness as 'very theatrical'. Olivier's statue stands nearby **12** But not everyone is a fan of Lasdun; in 1988 Prince Charles likened the building to 'a nuclear power station'.

with a programme ranging from dance to spoken word, and from pop to classical and world music. Now a grade I listed building, it was designed by Sir Leslie Martin. It is typical of 1950s modernism, with its emphasis on horizontal lines and an undecorated facade. Its curved roof nestled into the square foyer below has resulted in the affectionate nickname, the 'egg in a box'.

Continuing east, you meet the hulking concrete form of the Southbank Centre, the largest arts centre in the United Kingdom and home to galleries, performance spaces, cafes and restaurants. It was this development from the early 1960s that cemented the South Bank

Follow the Thames Path until you reach a kink that offers a spectacular view towards the City of London. Peer over the embankment walls and at low tide you can see Ernie's Beach, named after local Waterloo resident and activist John Hearn MBE (aka Ernie) in 2015. Ernie was a member of the social enterprise, the Coin Street Action Group, and in the 1970s campaigned for affordable housing and open space along the South Bank. It might not be white sand against sparkling blue sea, but it is thanks to him that we can enjoy this little slice of a beach in Central London.

From here you also get a good view of the former Oxo Tower Wharf, designed by AW Moore in 1928 for the Liebig Extract of Meat Company. There was actually a power station here previously, built around 1900, to generate electricity for the Royal Mail, but it is the remodelling that gives us the iconic glass panels spelling out 'OXO', a reference to the company's best-selling stock cube. Originally, Liebig wanted to have illuminated signage emblazoned with the brand, but their application was turned down due to advertising restrictions. No problem, thought the design team, instead incorporating the letters into the fabric of the building as architectural details. A sneaky loophole! The building was derelict by the 1970s and was bought

Opposite Royal Waterloo Hospital
for Children

by the Coin Street Community Builders, with major renovation starting in the 1990s. The result is a good example of a truly community-led development in London, with three floors of public space, a viewing gallery, retail space for designers and makers as well as 78 flats managed by a housing cooperative.

Head right through Gabriel's Wharf ⑬ Turn left onto Upper Ground, and then right into Bernie Spain Gardens. Originally an area of light-industrial warehouses, Gabriel's Wharf transformed into a collection of design-led shops in 1988 after a collaboration with Camden Lock Market. Laid out in the same year, Bernie Spain Gardens is named after local resident Bernadette Spain, who was a founding member of the Coin Street Action Group. Bernadette was pivotal in ensuring that this neighbourhood provided quality housing and open, public space for local residents as well as those visiting or working in the area.

Exit the gardens and turn right along Stamford Street. On the left is a residential terrace dating from the early 1800s, while on the right you will see the low-rise homes that are part of the Coin Street Development ⑭ Ahead is the Coin Street Action Group's neighbourhood centre, which provides

Gabriel's Wharf transformed into a collection of design-led shops in 1988 after a collaboration with Camden Lock Market.

community facilities including a nursery, youth clubs, weekend activities, meeting spaces and health services. As you pass further along Stamford Street the architecture moves from residential to commercial, with many of the 19th-century houses torn down in the early 1900s. At no. 127, on the left-hand side of the street, look up at the large cream building to see the letters 'WHS', right at the top above the main entrance. This was the printworks built by W H Smith & Son (1914–16). The building was sold to the *Daily Telegraph* in 1939 but never occupied thanks to the outbreak of the Second World War, and was used for storage instead. Today the buildings are part of King's College London.

Looming at the end of the street is the IMAX cinema, completed in 1999 and designed by English architect Bryan Avery. It houses the United Kingdom's largest cinema screen at 20 x 26m (65 x 85ft). Although you will be heading left, you may want to take a quick look at the surviving frontage of the Royal Waterloo Hospital for Children and Women, opposite the IMAX on Waterloo Road **15** Founded in 1816 in the City of London, a branch of the hospital was established here in the 1820s and this building dates from 1903–05. In its early years the Waterloo outpost was a dispensary, handing out medicine rather than providing in-patient care for children. Frustrated at the lack of facilities, one employee, Dr Charles West, would go on to establish Great Ormond Street Hospital in Bloomsbury, the first hospital in the United Kingdom dedicated solely to the care of children, which opened on Valentine's Day in 1852.

Follow the map past St John's Church, which you saw at the beginning of the walk, but now head through the church gardens. Converted into a garden in the 1870s, you can still see some of the remnants of the churchyard here, including tombs and the perimeter wall **16** Also dotted around the garden are more works from the London School of Mosaic, which is based in the crypt of the church. Its aim as a not-for-profit social enterprise is to make beautiful and skilful public art that enhances the environment while helping the homeless and local young people to learn new skills. The garden contains a memorial to, and sculpture garden for, local homeless people.

Exit the gardens onto Exton Street then turn right onto Cornwall Road. Look out for a blue plaque remembering Astley's Circus **17** Known as the father of the modern circus, Philip Astley put on a public spectacle here in 1768. Set amid the fields that still

characterized the area at the time, Philip and his wife Patty performed tricks on horseback, such as doing a handstand while riding, and picking up a handkerchief while steering a cantering horse. Gradually they added acrobats, clowns and other acts, so while the Astleys never in fact called it a 'circus' themselves, it is seen as a forerunner.

Cross Cornwall Road to enter Roupell Street. One of the most atmospheric streets in Waterloo, it was developed in the 1820s by John Palmer Roupell, a gold refiner. Now part of a conservation area, it is unsurprising that these stocky brickworkers' homes with their pitched roofs feature so often on

film and television ⑱ They have appeared in *Doctor Who*, *Legend* (starring Tom Hardy) and the James Bond film, *No Time To Die*.

Turn right onto Windmill Walk, making your way past the Kings Arms pub and then underneath the railway viaduct built in the 1860s. Continue to follow Windmill Walk until you reach The Cut. Laid out in 1798, The Cut was a new road that prompted the development of much of the area you have seen today.

Head left and you will soon see the colourful facade of the Young Vic Theatre ⑲ As you may have guessed, the Young Vic began as part of the Old Vic seen earlier on your

Opposite St John's Gardens
Right (top) Walklings Bakery plaque;
(bottom) 'Dog licking a bowl' sculpture

walk. Conceived as a place for new, unconventional and open theatre that was high quality but affordable, the company – led by Frank Dunlop – found a home here and opened with its first show in 1970.

The site, however, has a tragic backstory. On the corner once stood Walklings Bakery where – on 17 April 1941 – a bomb landed, killing the 54 people sheltering in the basement. It was one of the worst single disasters that the borough of Lambeth suffered during the Blitz. A small gold memorial plaque can be seen on Greet Street.

Continue along The Cut to reach Southwark Station where the tour ends ㉑ However, before you enter the station, you may want to cross the road and take a closer look at the curious sculpture diagonally opposite. Atop a lamppost is a strange sculpture of a dog licking a bowl ㉒ It is a replica of an ironmonger's shop sign that once stood here from the late 18th century until the 1930s. Charles Dickens – who would walk past it on his way to work in Charing Cross, aged 12, mentions it in a letter from which an excerpt has been reproduced on a panel on the floor.

IN FOCUS • COMMUNICATION

Whether it's posting a letter, making a phone call or sending a message to consumers, communication in a city needs to be eye-catching and efficient.

LET'S TAKE A CLOSER LOOK

Postboxes

A British icon, the red postbox actually started life as sage green. Anthony Trollope, later more famous as a novelist, worked at the Post Office in the 1850s and spearheaded the introduction of boxes into which people could post letters. Following initial trials in Jersey and Guernsey in 1852–3, postboxes were rolled out nationwide. Though they had been red during the trials, the colour green was chosen to make them less obtrusive on street corners. If anything, this was too subtle and after complaints they were difficult to find, in 1874 it was specified that all postboxes would be bright red. It took 10 years to repaint them all!

Telephone boxes

In 1924 the Royal Fine Arts Commission launched a competition to find a new design for telephone boxes. Sir Giles Gilbert Scott (1880–1960) designed the winning entry, deemed the most suitable by the General Post Office. Amazingly, Scott's original winning prototype can be found and admired today, behind the

Gold postboxes

As well as green and red, you can also find gold postboxes scattered around Greater London. They were painted to commemorate the London 2012 Olympics and its Gold Medal winners. The most central of these is on Tothill Street, Westminster, dedicated to London as the host city of the games.

entrance doors of Burlington House on Piccadilly.

There are two main types of red telephone box across the capital: the older K2 design, rolled out after 1926, and the updated K6 design from 1935. The K2 has equal-sized window panels, is much larger and has a perforated crown design, whereas the K6 has one larger middle glass panel and a slit below the word 'TELEPHONE', which acts as ventilation. The best place to play spot the difference is on Carey Street, Holborn, or along the Grand Avenue in Smithfield Market. Today some have been given a new lease of life, becoming mini cafes and libraries!

Police boxes
Police boxes enabled officers on their beat to call the station, transferring information more quickly than having to walk all the way back. They arrived in London from the late 1920s,

Opposite A standard double postbox **Left (top)** Telephone box library; **(bottom)** K2 and K6 side by side

having been pioneered in Sunderland in 1923, and the Metropolitan Police introduced the design by Gilbert Mackenzie Trench, made world famous as the TARDIS in *Doctor Who*. By the 1950s there were more than 650 police boxes across Greater London but improvements in radio technology meant they were no longer as useful. The last one standing, outside Earl's Court Station, dates from 1996 and was an attempt to improve the area and reduce crime by introducing a visible police presence and providing a base for officers.

More examples can be found in the City of London, although they look very different. The City of London has its own police force, established in 1832 and separate from the Metropolitan Police, which was established earlier, by Act of Parliament, in 1829. In this instance though, the City got here first, introducing 50 call boxes across the Square Mile from 1907. Today there are eight non-functional surviving ones, all repainted their original bright blue and dating from the 1920s or 1930s. They're all grade II listed by Historic England.

Ghost signs

'Ghost sign' is a term most commonly associated with large-scale, faded advertisements. However, a small proportion of these are non-commercial, functional signs that instruct or advise. Some of the most common examples include warnings to STICK NO BILLS or BILL STICKERS WILL BE PROSECUTED, informing would-be guerrilla advertisers that this is private property.

A more curiously worded sign is COMMIT NO NUISANCE,

which can be found on street corners, often beside churches that are within walking distance of pubs. The literal, non-euphemistic definition of this is essentially 'don't urinate here'. If the sign hasn't sufficiently deterred people, physical deflectors can also be spotted in corners, most notably by the Bank of England.

Other fairly common ghost signs are large 'S's, standing for air-raid shelters, which were used predominantly during the Second World War. Sometimes accompanied with an arrow and/or a written distance, a long form also exists, as stencilled proclamations of PUBLIC SHELTERS IN VAULTS UNDER PAVEMENTS IN THIS STREET. These communal shelters, made of several sheets of steel, were installed in parks or the basements of private homes, and could be used if you didn't have access to an Anderson shelter, or simply preferred to huddle in a warmer and less damp environment.

A number of ghost signs appear on the walks in this book, namely on pages 47, 127 (pictured top), 129, 146 and 178.

Opposite Police box
Above (top and bottom)
Ghost signs

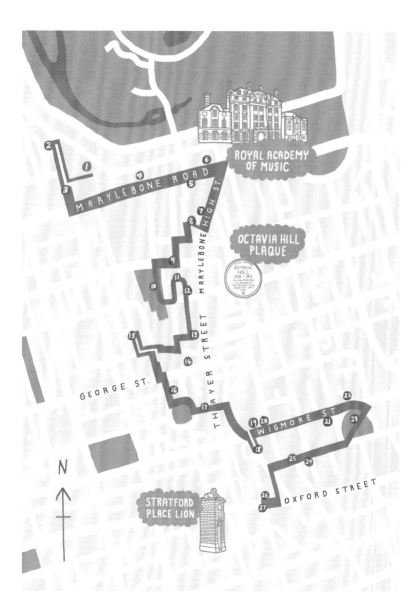

Marylebone walk

START
Baker Street London
Underground Station

FINISH
Bond Street London
Underground Station

DISTANCE
3.5km (2.2 miles)

In describing Marylebone's character, people often liken it to a little village nestled within Central London and, in a sense, it is just that. St Mary by the bourne (river) is an ancient part of London and takes its name from the old parish church and the River Tyburn. At its heart are Marylebone High Street and Marylebone Lane, the latter retaining its wiggly path north from Oxford Street.

The fields Marylebone Lane would have wound past are long gone, having been consumed by London's relentless drive for development. However, during the walk you will find plenty of places to appreciate the earlier charms of this neighbourhood, and to hear about its former residents.

The walk starts at Baker Street Station ❶ One of the earliest London Underground stations on the world's first underground railway, the Metropolitan Railway, Baker Street opened on 10 January 1863 and was the first station to be built almost entirely underground.

If arriving by Tube, exit via the signs for Baker Street (North) and then turn right out of the station. Shortly on your right you will see the entrance to Chiltern Court, a block of mansion flats designed by Charles Walter Clark in the late 1920s after the previous grand plans for a large hotel were interrupted by the First World War. To the left of the doors is a blue plaque erected by the Anglo-Norse Society. During the Second World War, buildings along Baker Street were used by the Special Operations Executive (SOE) to plan undercover sabotage missions in Nazi-occupied Europe. The main headquarters was at no. 64, further down Baker Street, but other buildings were used as well. In 1940 Prime Minister Winston Churchill had instructed the SOE to 'set Europe ablaze', and by 1945 there were a total of 13,000 male and female agents. One of their nicknames was the 'Baker Street Irregulars', a term first used by Arthur Conan Doyle in his Sherlock Holmes series to describe the young street urchins who were adept at finding out information and slipping about unnoticed. You will see more Sherlock connections shortly.

Cross the road to head north up Baker Street. Look up to admire Abbey House. In 2005 everything apart from the facade of this building was removed and it now contains Parkview Private Residences. However, a lighthouse sculpture and the word 'security' hint at the building's earlier function. Built in 1932, this was the headquarters of a building society founded in 1874. By 1944 it was known as Abbey National (bought by Santander in 2004), which provided insurance and banking services.

Continue up Baker Street to arrive at the Sherlock Holmes Museum ❷ Above the door you will spot a blue plaque declaring this as 221b Baker Street, despite the fact that it is actually no. 239. The museum was opened in 1990 by the Sherlock Holmes Society and for 15 years it lobbied Westminster Council to use 221b Baker Street as its official address. Strictly speaking, that address was on the site of Abbey House, which occupied 219–29 Baker Street. So seriously did Abbey National take this association with the fictional detective, that a woman called Erica Harper, who worked in PR, was given

the additional job of replying to Sherlock's fan mail, answering specific questions about cases or otherwise saying that Mr Holmes cannot comment as he has retired to Sussex, 'reviewing the records of his cases and keeping bees'. In 2005, when Abbey National closed, the museum won the right to use the address and now the Post Office recognizes this as 221b Baker Street.

Retrace your steps back down Baker Street and cross the road. Keep an eye out for the ghostly lettering above the newsagent at no. 194 ❸ Until it relocated to South Kensington in 2019, this was the home of Transport for London's Lost Property Office. If you have ever left an umbrella on the Tube, you are not alone. More than 1,000 items go missing on the network every day and, in the past, they all ended up here. A surprising 66 per cent of items are never recovered. **Continue down Baker Street, turning left at the corner, onto Marylebone Road.** Ahead, on the left, is a statue of Sherlock Holmes, sculpted by John Doubleday. Clad in his iconic cape and deerstalker, he smokes a pipe and appears deep in thought.

Ahead you will see the huge green dome of Madame Tussauds, the wax museum created by an extraordinary artist and businesswoman, Marie Grosholtz, born in 1761 ❹ Apprenticed from a very young age, Grosholtz was in France during the revolution and had the gruesome job of creating wax models of guillotined heads. When her master died, he left her everything and she travelled to London in the early 1800s, exhibiting her works. At a time before photography, these likenesses of famous faces must have awed their audiences, and her travelling displays proved popular. Grosholtz established a permanent museum on Baker Street in the 1830s (using her married name, Tussaud). She died in 1850, just before anyone could capture her in a photograph, so her likeness has fittingly only survived in a waxwork.

Cross over to the south side of Marylebone Road. Originally known as the New Road, this was laid out in 1757, cutting through fields to allow better driving of animals and linking the northern villages of Paddington, Marylebone and Islington. As with any major construction work in London, this project had its critics. The Duke of Bedford was thoroughly against the idea, fearing it would negatively affect his estate in Bloomsbury. Although Parliament approved the plan, the duke managed to guarantee that no building could be erected within 15m (50ft) of either side of the road. Almost a century later, when the rest of Britain was swept up with railway mania, a royal commission was established in 1846 and decided that no railway terminus should cross the boundary of the New Road. This is why the railway stations of Marylebone, Euston, St Pancras and Kings Cross all form a line beside each other, prohibited from penetrating further into Central London.

Stop on the corner of Nottingham Place. Look up above the entrance to the Methodist Church House to see a sculptural frieze from 1939, designed by David Evans. The main panel depicts Jesus recruiting some of his disciples, telling the fishermen that they could instead become fishers

Among the many items discarded on the Tube, some of the odder ones include a 40-inch television, a life-sized stuffed toy gorilla and even prosthetic limbs.

of men. The Methodist Missionary Society moved here in 1946.

Continue east along Marylebone Road. You will walk past the steps and columns of St Marylebone Parish Church, the fourth parish church to serve the area ❺ There is no St Marylebone – the area's name is a corruption of St Mary by the bourne. The building dates from c.1818 and was designed by Thomas Hardwick. Its most striking detail is the domed cupola supported by golden caryatids (female figures serving as columns). The earliest parish church, located on Oxford Street, was recorded in the 11th century and you will see the site of a second church – established around 1400 – shortly.

Left (top) Dickens frieze;
(bottom) Memorial Garden of Rest

Follow the map along **Marylebone Road, passing the Royal Academy of Music on the opposite side of the street** 6 Built 1910–11, the academy was founded in 1822, making it the oldest conservatoire in Britain. Famous alumni include the composer Arthur Sullivan, singer Katherine Jenkins, conductor Sir Simon Rattle and the singer/songwriter Sir Elton John.

Before turning right onto Marylebone High Street, pause to admire the 1960 sculptural frieze by Estcourt J Clack. It depicts a portrait of Charles Dickens and, within a thought bubble, some of the characters from his novels. Dickens lived on this site, the former no. 1 Devonshire Terrace, from 1839–51, but in the 1950s the houses were demolished. You might recognize a few of the characters shown here: Ebenezer Scrooge from A *Christmas Carol* and the eponymous David Copperfield. Towards the top of the frieze there is also a raven. Dickens kept a real pet raven called Grip who appears in his novel *Barnaby Rudge*.

Once on Marylebone High Street, on the left-hand side of the street you can spot a small square plaque. This is a reminder of Tyburn Manor House, mentioned in the Domesday Book of the 1080s. Sadly there are no records as to what it looked like in its early history but by the 1500s it had apparently been converted into a hunting lodge and a school. The manor house was finally demolished in 1791, having stood here for centuries, watching its rural surroundings slowly get swallowed up. As well as the contents of the plaque, the people who unveiled it also give us some clues to the development of Marylebone. You will hear more about the Howard de Walden Estate later on.

Continue down Marylebone High Street. You will pass St Marylebone Parish Church Gardens and shortly on your right you will see another little green space, today known as the Memorial Garden of Rest ❼ It was created in 1951 after a church that occupied this site was destroyed by a bomb in the Second World War. It was the second Marylebone Parish Church, built in 1740 to replace one founded here in 1400. By the early 1800s, this church was too small for the growing population of Marylebone and was replaced by the current St Marylebone. The building here survived as the parish chapel until it closed in 1926. The Garden of Rest contains some stone memorials, most notably to Charles Wesley and his wife Susanna. Charles was younger brother to the founder of the Methodist movement, John Wesley, and worked

alongside his brother writing lyrics for thousands of hymns including 'Hark! The Herald Angels Sing'.

Exit the gardens and walk a short distance along Marylebone High Street before turning right down the narrow Oldbury Place ❽ Laid out in 1892, this was largely home to small industrial sites – garages, builders and decorators. Today a renovated two-bedroom mews house can easily fetch £4 million. **Turn left, following Oldbury Place out onto Nottingham Street. Turn right onto Nottingham Street and then, after a short distance, left into Nottingham Place.** On leaving the low rise, cobbled mews streets the architecture changes into a lively mix of the shorter 18th-century homes with white stucco ground floors and taller 19th- and early-20th-century redbrick mansion blocks.

Look up towards Paddington Street and above no. 54 is the faded ghost sign of Edward Watson, a bookbinder who was based here 1870-81 ❾ **Turn right into Paddington Street and then cross into Paddington Street Gardens on your left** ❿ These were established in 1733, as extra burial grounds for the Marylebone Parish, but closed in 1814 and laid out as a public recreation ground in 1885. Most tombstones have been removed but the large, grade II listed, Fitzpatrick

Right Oldbury Place
Opposite Ragged and Industrial School

Family Mausoleum survives. It was erected in 1759 by Richard Fitzpatrick, son of the MP Richard Fitzpatrick, for his wife who died aged only 30.

Exit the gardens onto Moxon Street and turn left into Ossington Buildings. As well as the need for green, public space, a pressing issue in the 19th century was good-quality housing. While the Metropolitan Public Gardens Association (est. 1882) was the leading light in providing the former, the latter was a cause taken up by philanthropists and campaigners. In this case, Ossington Buildings were built in 1888 by the Portland Industrial Dwellings Company Limited, its initials visible above the doorways. They are named after Lady Ossington, co-owner of the Portland Estate. Rooms were in high demand, with only one third of prospective tenants successfully getting through the vetting process for proof of poverty and respectability. As well as the homes, there was a communal laundry whose chimney is still visible today and remembered in 'The Old Laundry' building. This development was a marked improvement on the slum housing here previously, described by the Vestry sanitary committee in 1847 as 'a miserable neighbourhood' and in 'the lowest stages of moral and physical degradation'.

Turn right and then left into the tiny Grotto Passage and look up at the whitewashed wall ⓫ The Ragged and Industrial School was established here in 1846 to save 'the ignorant and depraved youth of both sexes'. In a school converted from an old carpentry workshop, girls were taught needlework, reading and writing, while boys were occupied with mending clothes and boots, chopping firewood and making mattresses and hassocks (rough cushions). By 1860 the old workshop was falling apart so was rebuilt and enlarged. Throughout the ensuing decades the function and occupants of this establishment varied. It was sometimes used for schoolrooms or as a library, while at

other times it served as a large hall with hammocks hung out, providing an overnight shelter for the local homeless. This sounds bleak enough, but was marginally better than the situation before, a series of courts with ramshackle housing crammed full of as many people as the immoral landlords could squeeze in. In 1858 there was a shocking case of an elderly man and his two grown-up children living in a single room – only fit for one person – alongside a couple, the woman lying dead and her husband only barely alive.

Backtrack through Grotto Passage and follow the map into Garbutt Place. Above no. 2 you can see a blue plaque to Octavia Hill **12** Born in 1838,

in Cambridgeshire, Hill's parents were keen social reformers, establishing a local infant school that also served as a community centre in the evenings.

Although her upbringing was initially comfortable, Hill's father's business failed and after falling into depression he abandoned the family, leaving Octavia's mother, Caroline, to ensure the family's survival. They moved to North London and, from the age of 14, Octavia worked in a Ragged School for Girls managed by her mother. It would set her up for a lifetime of work trying to improve the lives of London's poor and vulnerable. Within the family network of radical social reformers, Octavia used her connections to buy

Right (top) Garbutt Place; **(bottom)** Daunt Books

Right (top) Garbutt Place; **(bottom)** Daunt Books

and manage properties on this street, formerly Paradise Place. Described by her biographer as a 'friendly face of landlordism', Octavia was strict but showed compassion and respect to her tenants. By 1874 she was managing the housing of more than 3,000 people across London.

Leave Garbutt Place, crossing Moxon Street and head down Cramer Street. If you have time and the inclination, you may want to take a short detour onto Marylebone High Street to visit Daunt Books, an exquisite book shop over three floors at nos 83–4. Established by James Daunt in 1989, and specializing in travel books, there has been a book shop on the site of no. 83 since 1860, first managed by Francis Edwards. Edwards' son – also named Francis – rebuilt the shop in 1908, expanding next door and employing W. Henry White to create an extravagant but homely interior. It remained in the Edwards family until the late 1970s.

To continue with the walk, head down Cramer Street. Look up ahead to see the redbrick building of St Vincent's Roman Catholic Primary School, with the unusual addition of a playground on its roof ⓭ **Turn right onto St Vincent Street and then left into Aybrook Street.** Suddenly appearing like a grey, spiky prehistoric monster is St James's Roman Catholic Church ⓮ The current building was designed by competition winner Edward Goldie, influenced by early-13th-century English Gothic cathedrals such as Salisbury and Westminster Abbey. It opened in 1890, replacing a Spanish chapel, built in 1793 and designed by Joseph Bonomi (coincidentally the great-grandfather of Goldie). Bonomi's first chapel was built shortly after the Catholic Relief Act of 1791, relieving some of the restrictions on Catholic worship. Until 1827 (when the church fell under the control of London Vicariate, today the Diocese of Westminster), the church had a close relationship with the Spanish embassy, based in Manchester Square, which you will see shortly, and remembered in the nearby street, Spanish Place. If you'd like to see inside, the main entrance can be found on George Street.

Turn right onto Blandford Street, crossing Manchester Street and then turn right into Chiltern Street. Dominating the street is the red and white Chiltern Firehouse, a restaurant and 26-bedroom hotel ⓯ Unsurprisingly, this was once an actual fire station, Manchester Square Fire Station built in 1889. Despite the conversion, lovely details have been retained including the lettering,

overhanging fire lamp and carvings of helmet-wearing, moustachioed firemen. But the most intriguing survivor is the delicate neo-Gothic turret, a former watchtower, handy for spotting nearby fires. Opposite Chiltern Firehouse is Monocle Cafe (featured on page 153).

Retrace your steps back along Blandford Street. Look up above no. 48 to see a brown plaque commemorating Michael Faraday (1791–1867), known as the father of electricity because of his work building the world's first electric generator in 1831. **Turn right onto Manchester Street.** Here, you are tracing the edge of the Wallace Collection, a gem of a museum that is free to visit ⓰ It has a staggering collection of Sèvres porcelain, armour and paintings by artists including Rembrandt, Rubens, Canaletto and van Eyck.

Make your way to the front of the museum, and turn to face Manchester Square. From this vantage point it is easier to appreciate the fact that the Wallace Collection was once a grand country house, built for the Duke of Manchester in 1776. The 2nd Marquess of Hertford bought the leasehold in 1797 and it was renamed Hertford House. The collection is named after Sir Richard

Left (top) St James's Church;
(bottom) Chiltern Firehouse

Wallace, son of the 4th Marquess of Hertford, who inherited his father's love of art and collecting. Richard renovated the building, adding a large extension in the 1870s, and left it all to his wife on his death. When she died, it was left to the nation and it opened to the public in 1990.

Exit Manchester Square onto Hinde Street. Above no. 11 is a blue plaque to Rose Macaulay ⓱ Macaulay published 23 novels during her lifetime and lived in this flat from 1941, having been bombed out of her first Marylebone flat on Luxborough Street. It was here that she wrote her most famous novel, *The Towers of Trebizond*, which surely has one of the best opening lines of a novel: '"Take my camel, dear" said my Aunt Dot, as she climbed down from the animal on her return from High Mass.'

Continue along Hinde Street, passing Hinde Street Methodist Church on your left. Built 1881–7, and designed by James Weir, its off-centre tower and spire to the left of the triangular pediment looks a little odd. In fact, there was meant to be a matching one on the opposite corner to balance it out but for some reason it never materialized.

Cross Mandeville Place and continue along Hinde Street until you reach Marylebone Lane and turn

Left The Wallace Collection

from 1776 serves as a visual clue of this history. The land owned by the City was known as the Conduit Mead Estate, originally a 27-acre site. You will see some further reminders of this later on the walk.

Return to Wigmore Street and cross back over to the north side of the street for a closer look at John Bell & Croyden ⑲ In 1798 John Bell opened a pioneering pharmacy on Oxford Street, making each prescription onsite. His son, Jacob, would go on to found the Pharmaceutical Society in 1841 and the company received its first royal warrant in 1909. Three years later the company moved to this location on Wigmore Street. Inside are small cases displaying heritage items from its collection, including a prescription book from 1902 with all the medication ordered by the royal household. The company also claims to have the secret recipe and a sample of the holy oil used during the Coronation ceremony for the monarch.

Wigmore Street takes its name from a village and castle in Herefordshire, which Queen Elizabeth I (r. 1558–1603) sold to a Thomas Harley in 1601. This might seem bizarre, but it is just one of many historic links with the owner of the land in this area of the West

right. The narrow, winding street is very much the same as it would have been hundreds of years ago, its irregular path determined by the River Tyburn that still flows under your feet today. **Follow Marylebone Lane to reach Wigmore Street and cross the street.** Shortly on the left, embedded near the floor in a modern building is a plaque confirming the site of a conduit belonging to the City of London ⑱ The City bought land here in 1237 when constructing the Great Conduit, a system of piping fresh water around 4.8km (3 miles) under London to a public tap on Cheapside. The pipe was destroyed during the Great Fire of 1666 and never rebuilt, however this commemorative plaque

End. To explain fully, we need a bit of context. Cavendish Square (visited shortly) was the centrepiece of the development initiated by Edward Harley, 2nd Earl of Oxford, in 1717. Harley married Lady Henrietta Cavendish Holles, and their daughter, Margaret, married the 2nd Duke of Portland. The estate was known as the Portland Estate until 1879 when the 5th Duke, having no heirs, passed the land to his sister, widow of the 6th Baron Howard de Walden. The Howard de Walden Estate took ownership of around 200 acres of real estate and, despite the estate being half the size today, it was still worth an estimated £4.7 billion as of 2020.

By the early 1900s, Wigmore Street was known as a location for high-end shopping with cafes, antique stores, multiple opticians and businesses specializing in the sale of medical and surgical equipment. The grandeur and optimism of the street can be seen in no. 33, built 1906–7 as the headquarters of Debenham & Freebody drapers ㉒ Designed by architects William Wallace and James Gibson, the facade is covered with Carrara marble tiles and the original interior continued on a luxury theme inside, covered with grey and green marble. When the store opened, its manager declared it 'the most comfortable shop in the world' and in 1925 it was a very early pioneer of the onsite underground car park, with space for more than 100 cars and an indicator board that alerted chauffeurs when their clients were ready to leave! Debenhams sold the premises in 1981 and it has since been redeveloped, the facade and external features preserved with a grade II listing.

Continue on Wigmore Street until you reach Cavendish Square. On the corner, at no. 17 (built 1756), is a good example of a fine terraced house intended to populate the square ㉑ It has some fun neoclassical details that were added by Gilbert Hayes in the 20th century: 'graces' (Greek goddesses) are flanked by pilasters (flat columns), while a frieze of putti (wingless cherubs) play in an orchestra. The musical references are here because the building housed John Brinsmead & Sons Ltd, piano-makers, which moved here 1923–4. Today it functions as serviced office space.

After laying out Cavendish Square in 1717, building work took a few decades to complete but it nevertheless attracted peers, politicians and wealthy businessmen. **Stay on the north side of the square and you will shortly reach Dean's Mews, with a dramatic stone archway affixed with a large**

Right (top) Debenham and Freebody; **(bottom)** 17 Cavendish Square

sculpture ㉒ The whole north section of this square was originally intended as one house for the Duke of Chandos. However, the South Sea Bubble financial crash in 1720 put an end to such grand plans; the duke bought the freehold of the site and more modest houses were planned, but nothing happened until 1769 when George Foster Tufnell MP built the houses here and this mews appeared. From 1889 the buildings were occupied by the Convent of the Holy Child of Jesus, and after bomb damage in the Second World War they commissioned the stone bridge linking their buildings.

The arch was designed by Louis Osman, who also wanted a sculpture to fill the space and approached Jacob Epstein to create a Madonna and Child, recycling the lead from the bombed roof. It may not seem provocative today, but this was a very early depiction of highly Catholic iconography in a bold and very public place. There is a story associated with this artwork, that the nuns were shocked when the identity of the artist was revealed (Epstein was born in New York to Jewish émigré parents). It is claimed that the convent baulked and cancelled the commission. However, there is also evidence that they were nothing but thrilled with the final piece, visiting Epstein in his studio.

He recalls 'they showed the warmest interest in the work and asked to be allowed to contemplate it quietly and alone for some time'. Both accounts might be true, of course, the Mother Superior being first surprised by the choice and then converted when seeing the artwork in the flesh. In 1969 Heythrop College moved to this site, and since 1995 it has been home to the King's Fund, an independent health charity.

Head into the centre of Cavendish Square to find the site of another controversial sculpture, of which only the plinth remains ㉓ This once held an equestrian statue of Prince William Augustus, Duke of Cumberland, and youngest son of King George II (r. 1727–60). Unveiled in 1770 'in honour to his public virtue', so the plinth says, the duke was most famous for his brutal victory at the Battle of Culloden in 1746. He led an army on behalf of the British government against the Jacobite forces intent on restoring the Stuart kings on the throne. The last pitched battle on British soil, taking place in the Scottish highlands, the event saw the Jacobites outnumbered and thousands were slaughtered. The statue was taken down in 1868 and never replaced.

In 2012, it became the site of an unusual contemporary artwork, a copy of the statue but in soap, intended to dissolve away in the London rain and designed by Korean sculptor

Opposite (left) Dean's Mews;
(right) Stratford Place

Meekyoung Shin. Her eerie work survived until 2016 when the final misshapen remnants were removed.

Exit Cavendish Square onto Henrietta Place. Here, you will see the large department stores of John Lewis and House of Fraser, which occupy the austere art deco mass of 318 Oxford Street, dating from 1935–7. Providing a stark contrast next door is St Peter Vere Street, built 1721–4 to serve the newly laid out Cavendish Square **24** Designed by James Gibbs, it is said to have been a mini precursor to his more famous church, St Martin-in-the-Fields, in Trafalgar Square.

Continuing the architectural theme, on the right-hand side of the street is Henrietta House, headquarters of the CBRE Group, an American property and investment company since 2011 **25** Though renovated, the building has retained 15 Portland stone sculptures by Keir Smith, dating from 1991. They chart the architectural history of Britain and include landmark buildings such as St Paul's Cathedral, Senate House Library and One Canada Square.

At the end of Henrietta Place, turn left so that you are back on Marylebone Lane. Here, you can admire the brick rear facades and scattered windows of grand houses that front the street parallel to this

one: Stratford Place. **Take the right fork in the road to reach busy Oxford Street, formerly known as Tyburn Road.** If you were to continue west, you would reach Marble Arch. Named after the stone triumphal arch moved here in 1850, it was once the site of Tyburn Tree, London's major site of public hangings until 1783.

On a cheerier note, step into Stratford Place and look up at the stone pillar on your right **26** This lion was once one of a pair that flanked a gated, residential community first laid out by Edward Stratford in the 1770s. Stratford leased the land from the City of London as it was part of the aforementioned Conduit Mead Estate and, specifically, the site of a banqueting house built for the Lord Mayor of London in 1565. Thirteen of the original 22 houses survive, including the grandest, Stratford House (since 1962, the Oriental Club) at the end of the road.

Turn back towards Oxford Street, where you will find multiple entrances to Bond Street Station **27**

TOP 10 · GREEN SPACES

Although it might not always feel like it, London is a surprisingly green city with more than eight million trees and 12,800 green, open spaces. Here are some of the quirkier ones to enjoy across the capital.

1. The Pergola, Hampstead Heath, NW3

Within the 800 acres of Hampstead Heath, one of the prettiest corners is The Pergola, originally a private Italianate garden created for William Lever in 1904. The London County Council bought it in 1963 and it has since been open to the public.

2. Streatham Rookery, Streatham Common, SW16

The Rookery, as it was known in the 18th century, was once a large house surrounded by gardens and the Streatham Springs, a place for Londoners to enjoy a health retreat. Under threat of redevelopment in 1912, it was saved by a local resident, Stenton Covington.

3. Postman's Park, EC1

One of more than 375 green spaces within the Square Mile, Postman's Park is next to the former offices of the General Post Office and is on the site of the former churchyard of St Botolph's, Aldersgate. It also contains a memorial with plaques celebrating the everyday heroism of Londoners from the late 19th and early 20th centuries.

4. Redcross Gardens, SE1

This quaint little garden, overlooked by cottages, was a flagship project for Octavia Hill, philanthropist and co-founder of the National Trust. First opened in 1887 the garden was restored to its Victorian plan in 2005.

5. Barbican Conservatory, EC2

A hidden gem, the Barbican Centre's conservatory was designed as a green respite for residents in 1984 but can be visited by anyone for free.

6. Isabella Plantation, Richmond Park, KT2

A gated garden within Richmond Park, this is beautiful all year round but is particularly bursting with colour during late April to early May when the azaleas are in bloom.

7. Kyoto Garden, Holland Park, W11

Set within the 54-acre Holland Park, the Kyoto Garden opened in 1991, a gift to mark London's Japan festival the following year.

8. The Garden at 120, EC3

The largest public roof terrace in the City, the Garden at 120 Fenchurch Street opened in 2019 and is a free viewing platform with no prebooking needed.

9. Tower Hamlets Cemetery, E3

One of London's 'Magnificent Seven' cemeteries, built to combat the problem of Central London's overcrowded cemeteries. With more than 250,000 people interred beneath your feet it's impossible not to feel the history walking through this wonderfully atmospheric and overgrown nature reserve.

10. Brown Hart Gardens, W1

You would probably never guess that Brown Hart Gardens is on top of an electricity substation. Surrounded by mansion blocks and a beautiful Catholic church, this raised garden is the perfect place to escape the busy Oxford Street, just minutes away.

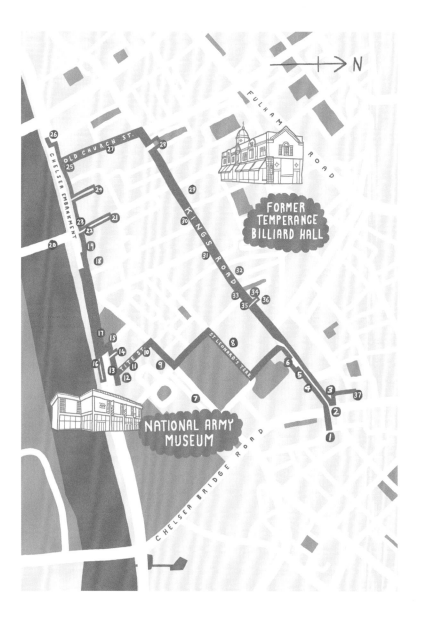

Chelsea walk

START
Sloane Square London
Underground Station

FINISH
Sloane Square London
Underground Station

DISTANCE
4.9km (3 miles)

Of all the walks in this book, this one gives you the best 'escape' from Central London. This is thanks to Chelsea's history. For most of its existence Chelsea was a separate riverside village and the area still retains that character, with references to rural lanes and historic country homes. The name comes from the Anglo-Saxon word for chalk, *cealc*, and island, *ey* or *ea*.

Things started changing for the sleepy riverside village from the 18th century. It is estimated that, in 1703, Chelsea had around 300 houses, but by 1801 there was a population of 12,000. This rapid growth continued into the 19th century with the population growing from around 40,000 by 1841 to 88,000 just 40 years later.

Opposite Venus Fountain,
Sloane Square

Your walk begins in the bustling heart of Sloane Square ❶ But if you have arrived on the Tube, take a moment to look up along the platforms before you exit the station. A large sewer pipe hanging over the tracks carries the 'lost' River Westbourne – which rises in Hampstead and empties by Chelsea Bridge – over your head!

Exit Sloane Square Station to arrive in Sloane Square. Laid out in the late 18th century, it is now populated with mainly 19th- and 20th-century buildings. Cross into the paved centre of the square to get a closer look at the Venus Fountain, made in 1953 by Chelsea-born sculptor Gilbert Ledward ❷ The statue depicts a kneeling figure, eyes looking demurely down, surmounting a carved vase-like base. Around the large bronze base is a shallow relief of King Charles II (r. 1660–85) and Nell Gwyn, his favourite mistress (see page 72), sitting by the banks of the Thames as a swan swims past. In a way, the fountain sets the tone for your walk and the area, a focus on arts and beauty as well as an appreciation for nature and connections with royals and celebrities.

The west side of Sloane Square is dominated by the grade II* listed facade of Peter Jones, now part of John Lewis & Partners, built 1935–7

❸ Perhaps a more likeable version of a harsh modern block, its delicate vertical lines and friendly curve along the King's Road make it less of an eyesore for those against 20th-century architecture.

Exit Sloane Square along the King's Road. Originally a private royal road constructed for King Charles II, it was laid out in the late 17th century for easy access between London and Hampton Court Palace. Opposite the far corner of Peter Jones, take a look left into Duke of York Square and you will see an animated statue of a boy leaping over a bollard by Allister Bowtell ❹ It is a playful reference to a school whose former building you will see shortly.

Follow the map a short way along King's Road until you reach the large public space of Duke of York Square. It stands on the site of a school for military orphans built in 1801. The main building is now occupied by the Saatchi Gallery, a contemporary art gallery, seen beyond the curtain wall ahead. The school building was bought by Cadogan Group Ltd in 1998, a property developer and one of the major landowners who manage almost 100 acres in Chelsea today. The Cadogan family first gained a foothold in Chelsea in 1717 with a savvy marriage between Charles, 2nd

Right (top) Saatchi Gallery; **(bottom)** Hans Sloane statue

Baron Cadogan, and Elizabeth Sloane, daughter of Hans Sloane whose statue can be seen in the square **5** Hans Sloane bought the manor of Chelsea in 1712 as well as Beaufort House, the remnants of which you will see later on. Sloane Square – and plenty more local streets – are named after him.

Hans Sloane is most famous as the founding father of the British Museum. When he died, in 1753, he left his vast collection of over 71,000 specimens, books and objects to King George II (r. 1727–60) for the nation, stipulating that these be made accessible in a new and freely open museum. An avid collector, it was while working as private physician to the governor of Jamaica that Sloane's interest in natural history was piqued.

It was also in Jamaica that Sloane observed local people drinking a liquid made from the cocoa plant. Although nauseating at first, when it was mixed with milk, he found that he liked the taste and in bringing this concoction back to England, he is credited as the inventor of drinking chocolate. The recipe was later sold to Messrs Cadbury in the 19th century. On his return to England, Sloane married the wealthy heiress Elizabeth Langley Rose, whose family had made their fortune through slave-run sugar plantations in Jamaica.

Right (top) Duke of York Square;
(bottom) 18 St Leonard's Terrace

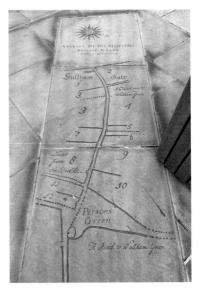

Follow the map across Duke of York Square and look down. Carved into the stone floor is a reminder of the history of the King's Road, shown as a rural track, looking like an ancient bus route, with the old place names on either side ❻ Surrounding the carving you will see small coins embedded into the pavement, replicas of tokens that would have been used to gain access to the private road.

Exit Duke of York Square onto Cheltenham Terrace, and turn left. Through the railings here you get a good view of the Saatchi Gallery mentioned earlier. Turn right onto St Leonard's Terrace. Shortly, on your left, you will see the enclosed green space and, beyond, the redbrick buildings of the Royal Hospital ❼ Built 1682–91, and designed by Christopher Wren, the hospital arose from a need to care for army veterans following the English Civil War in the mid-1600s. Influenced by the Hôtel des Invalides in Paris, Charles II issued a royal warrant to establish a centre of care for those 'broken by age or war'.

Today the building is still home to the Chelsea Pensioners. To apply, you have to be a former soldier of the British Army, be over 65 years of age, have no dependents and forego your pension. Women have been accepted since 2009.

Left Oscar Wilde's plaque at no. 34 Tite Street

admire a closer view of the Royal Hospital buildings.

Turn right onto Royal Hospital Road. Shortly, on your left, you will see the National Army Museum, which examines the role of the army from the 17th century to the present day **9** The modern museum stands on the site of the home of Sir Robert Walpole, Britain's first prime minister. Built in 1690, and made part of the Royal Hospital in the 18th century, it was destroyed by a land mine in April 1941.

Follow the map to turn left into Tite Street. It was developed in the 1870s as a purpose-built community of artists' studio-homes. Look out for the blue plaque at no. 34 dedicated to Oscar Wilde **10** He moved into the house in 1885 while at the height of his fame, and it was here that he wrote *The Picture of Dorian Gray* and *The Importance of Being Earnest*. Wilde lived here for around 10 years and used to write in a room overlooking the street. It was also from here that he was led to jail, convicted of gross indecency after a trial in which his former lover, Lord Alfred Douglas, gave evidence of their intimate relationship. Homosexuality wouldn't be legal in Britain until the passing of the Sexual Offences Act in 1967.

The American artist John Singer Sargent also lived on Tite Street, at

Continue along St Leonard's Terrace until you reach no. 18. Look up to see a blue plaque commemorating the fact that Bram Stoker, author of *Dracula*, lived here in the 1890s **8** **Turn left down Durham Place.** Built in 1790, the name is a nod to Durham House, which stood here in the late 1600s and is thought originally to have been a tavern called Ship House, built for workmen constructing the Royal Hospital. In 2020 nos 2–3, previously one dwelling, collapsed during extensive basement excavations. Townhouses along Durham Place cost £6 million, on average. **Continue straight on from Durham Place into Ormonde Gate.** At the corner of Royal Hospital Road, no. 31 ⓫ One of his most famous paintings is of the actress Ellen Terry depicted in her role as Lady Macbeth, draped in a rich robe of green, blue and gold, her deep red hair impossibly long in two braided pieces. She lifts a crown above her head in poised victory and the painting is captivating; you can see it for free at Tate Britain.

The painting was completed in Sargent's Tite Street studio and, in a nice coincidence, Oscar Wilde had actually seen Terry's performance and was spellbound. So, what a surprise that Lady Macbeth, in full costume and ready to pose for Sargent, should pass his window! Wilde wrote of Tite Street that, 'The street that on a wet and dreary morning has vouchsafed the vision of Lady Macbeth in full regalia magnificently seated in a four-wheeler can never again be as other streets: it must always be full of wonderful possibilities.'

No. 35 was occupied by the painter Rex Whistler ⓬ Chelsea had already been a popular haunt of creatives, but it was Whistler's move here that provoked a flurry of others to follow suit, including Sargent.

Before reaching Chelsea Embankment, turn right off Tite Street and into Dilke Street. At no. 7 is the London Sketch Club, a lasting reminder of Chelsea's artistic history, which was founded in 1898 and is a private members' club for artists ⓭ Further along to your right, have a look along Clover Mews ⓮ With its cobbled street and low-rise modest houses, this is a reminder that these once served as stables and provided staff accommodation for the local grand houses.

Exit Dilke Street onto Swan Walk. The wall ahead of you encircles Chelsea Physic Garden, the second-oldest botanical garden in England (the first is in Oxford) ⓯ Founded by the Society of Apothecaries in 1673, it owes its continued existence to Hans Sloane who donated the freehold of the land in 1772. It contains more than 5,000 species of plants – including the world's northernmost grapefruit growing outdoors – as well as the earliest surviving rock garden in England, built in 1772. If you would like to visit, the main entrance is on Cheyne Place, around to your right.

To continue the walk, follow the map left onto Chelsea Embankment ⓰ As you saw on the Westminster walk, Joseph Bazalgette reclaimed 22 acres of land from the Thames in order to upgrade London's sewer network in the late 19th century. Chelsea Embankment was created as a new road and pleasant promenade along the river. From here you can see

Opposite Albert Bridge
Right Golden Peace Pagoda,
Battersea Park

across the River Thames to Battersea Park, admiring the view of the Golden Peace Pagoda, built in 1984. The pagoda was a gift from Nichidatsu Fujii, a Japanese Buddhist monk, who, from 1947 decided to construct peace pagodas across the world in the name of world peace.

Continue west along the embankment. Shortly you can enjoy a view into the Chelsea Physic Garden through some railings ⑰ Look up to see the coat of arms of the Worshipful Society of Apothecaries. Flanked by unicorns, you see the Greek god Apollo, who represents healing, killing the dragon of disease. At the top is a rhinoceros, included because of the mistaken belief that their horns were medicinal.

A little further along the embankment, turn right and then left onto Cheyne Walk. This is one of the most illustrious addresses in Chelsea, and you will find a number of blue plaques to former residents. At no. 4, author Mary Ann Evans – pen name George Eliot – lived here for only a few weeks before dying of a chill in 1880. Further along the street at no. 16 is the former home of the Pre-Raphaelite artist Dante Gabriel Rossetti ⑱ As well as creating some of the most recognizable paintings of the 20th century, it was at this home that

Rossetti housed his eclectic animal menagerie including an owl, peacocks, kangaroo, racoon and the artist's beloved pet wombat.

Towards the end of the street, keep your eyes peeled for a small path on your right, Cheyne Mews, where you will see a blue information plaque about King Henry VIII's Manor House ⑲ Built in 1536 as a wedding present to the monarch's last wife, Katherine Parr, and later becoming home to his children, the future King Edward VI (r. 1547–53) and Queen Elizabeth I (r. 1558–1603), the house was demolished in 1753 after the death of Hans Sloane (its final resident).

As you reach Oakley Street, you will get a view of Albert Bridge ⑳

One of the prettiest bridges spanning the River Thames, it opened in 1873. Its elegance is reflected in its nickname 'The Trembling Lady', and there is a sign informing soldiers to break step while crossing as the vibrations were causing damage and a threat of collapse. Before crossing Oakley Street, music fans might like to take a short detour up the street to see the blue plaque at no. 42 **21** Unveiled in 2019 it commemorates Bob Marley who lived here in 1977 while writing the album *Exodus* with his band The Wailers, having recently left Jamaica following an assassination attempt. As well as the title track 'Exodus', the album also included the song 'Jamming'.

Back on Cheyne Walk, on the corner of Oakley Street is a delightful sculpture that appears to defy gravity. It is called *Boy with Dolphin* by David Wynne and was unveiled in 1975 **22** A self-taught artist who had previously studied zoology, Wynne based the figure on his nine-year-old son. Look across Chelsea Embankment towards the river and you can see a dilapidated green shed, one of 13 remaining – and protected – Cabmen Shelters. Established in 1875, they provided Hackney carriage drivers with a hot meal or drink, and some are still public cafes. **23**

Continue along Cheyne Walk and then turn right up Cheyne Row. You will shortly reach Carlyle's House, owned by the National Trust and former home of the Scottish historian and writer Thomas Carlyle, who lived here from 1834 until his death in 1881 **24** Most famous for his history of the French Revolution, despite being highly regarded in his lifetime and celebrated as the 'Sage of Chelsea', Carlyle held deeply anti-Semitic and racist views, writing a pamphlet in 1849 titled 'Occasional Discourse on the Negro Question' in which he insulted the appearance and intelligence of Black Africans. Slavery had been abolished within the British Empire in 1833, so his views were met with widespread disapproval at the time. **Return to Cheyne Walk.** Here, you will see a statue of a pensive-looking Carlyle on the green looking out to the Thames.

Turn right to continue along Cheyne Walk, heading towards Chelsea Old Church **25** Before you reach the church, you will find the elaborate tomb of Hans Sloane, surrounded by railings. Continue along the narrow path with the railings on your right, and shortly on your left is the back of another statue, this time of Thomas More. More was a wealthy and successful lawyer in

Left (top) Hans Sloane Mausoleum; **(bottom)** Chelsea Old Church

the 16th century, buying Beaufort Manor House in 1520. In 1529 he was appointed Lord Chancellor to King Henry VIII (r. 1509–47), but in only a few short years had fallen foul of the king over their differing religious beliefs and was beheaded on Tower Hill in 1535.

From the outside, Chelsea Old Church doesn't seem old at all and, in fact, it was heavily restored after catastrophic bomb damage in 1941. However, if you are able to go inside, you will find the homely interior of a village parish church, with much of its eastern end surviving from as far back as the 13th century as well as several 17th-century monuments.

Cross Old Church Street to walk through the sunken Roper's Gardens, and towards what looks like an ancient Tudor palace ㉖ This is Crosby Moran Hall, named after Sir John Crosby, who, in 1466, built this house on Bishopsgate, east of the City of London. The house was moved – piece by piece – to its current riverside location in 1910, having stood in the City for almost 500 years and been home to King Richard III (r. 1483–85) and Thomas More. It has been heavily restored since the 1980s, but still contains the authentic 15th-century Great Hall roof and is grade II* listed. Today it is the private home

of Dr Christopher Moran, chairman
of Co-Operation Ireland.

**Walk back through Roper's
Gardens and turn left up Old Church
Street.** At no. 46, look up to see a
terracotta cow's head protruding from
the building ㉗ This, along with some
attractive painted tiles, tells you that
it is the former Wright's Dairy, one of
the earliest in Chelsea, which from
the late 1700s had around 50 grazing
cows. Wright's lasted as a business
into the early 20th century and was
eventually bought by United Dairies.
However, you can still see multiple
cows' heads along the King's Road
commemorating the history.

**Continue on Old Church Street
until you reach the King's Road and
turn right.** Crossing the road, take a
detour through Carlyle Square ㉘ Laid
out in the 1860s, and named after
Thomas who you met earlier, its tall
trees provide a buffer from the busy
King's Road. **Rejoin the King's Road
and continue.** Shortly, on your left,
you will see the attractive green space
of Dovehouse Green, the former
burial ground for Chelsea Old Church,
with a number of large monuments
scattered across the green ㉙ It
closed for burials in 1882. Across the
road, a little further up on the right,
is Chelsea Old Town Hall, built in
stages from the late 1800s to early

1900s **30** It was the headquarters of the Metropolitan Borough of Chelsea from 1900, but since 1965, with the creation of the Royal Borough of Kensington and Chelsea, it is mainly used as an events venue. It has hosted many a celebrity wedding, including that of Wallis Simpson and her first husband; Bobby and Tina Moore; Marc Bolan and June Child; and Hugh Grant and Anna Eberstein.

Further along King's Road, at nos 131–41 on your right, you will see the striking green tiles and unusual shape of the former Temperance Billiard Hall **31** Built 1912–14, it was one of many halls constructed by Temperance Billiards Halls Ltd to promote more wholesome leisure

activities as an alternative to the consumption of alcohol. The billiard hall closed in the 1960s and became an antiques centre; it is now a shop. You might want to pop inside to admire the surviving interior features.

A short walk ahead on your left is another unusual building, known as the Pheasantry, and today used as a restaurant **32** It is a flamboyant display of classical architecture, including a triumphal arch topped with a quadriga (four horses pulling a chariot) and two supporting caryatids (women used as columns). It was once the home of artist and interior decorator Amédée Joubert, who used it as his showroom. The name was established from the previous owner,

Bottom Wright's Dairy cow
Opposite Bywater Street

Samuel Baker, who sold birds here from the late 1700s to the mid-1860s.

Follow the map up King's Road until you reach two plaques celebrating two women. The first, a couple of houses into Smith Street, at no. 50, honours PL Travers ㉝ Born in Australia as Helen Lyndon Goff, she is most famous for creating the character of Mary Poppins. First published in 1934, Goff intended the story for an adult audience and always resented Disney's sugar-coating of the tale for its film in 1964.

Back on the other side of King's Road, look up above no. 138A for a plaque to Mary Quant, the clothing designer who made the King's Road a fashion destination when her shop Bazaar opened in 1955 ㉞ Credited with introducing the mini skirt, Quant disrupted women's fashion forever. Her shop turned heads with its lurid window displays of bold prints and bright colours, oversized floppy hats and thigh-high patent boots, and caused the young and the cool to flock to the King's Road during the 'Swinging Sixties'. Opposite, at no. 69, look up to spot a reminder of Wright's Dairy with another of the historic cows' heads that look down on Chelsea ㉟

Take the next left off King's Road, Bywater Street, to enter a lovely,

colourful dead end ㊱ This is one of London's photogenic 'rainbow' streets. There is no real reason behind them, other than residents decide among themselves to paint their houses, sometimes discussing colour choices with one another as part of the planning.

Return to the King's Road, and from here it is a short walk back to Sloane Square Station where the walk ends. There are plenty of places to stop for refreshment, but perhaps the nicest location is Pavilion Road, a newly renovated pedestrian street, redeveloped by the Cadogan Estate and part of the Hans Town Conservation Area ㊲ **To reach it, head left onto Cadogan Gardens, then turn right onto Symons Street and turn left into Pavilion Road.**

IN FOCUS • STREET FURNITURE

Bollards, streetlights and benches are so ubiquitous in cities that we tend to pass by without taking much notice, especially if they serve a function.

LET'S TAKE A CLOSER LOOK

Nothing makes it onto the streets of London without at least some thought and consideration behind it.

Bollards

There is an urban myth that all London bollards are made from French cannon stolen during the Battle of Trafalgar, but it is simply not true. In fact, no French ship from Trafalgar was ever brought back to England.

There are some – rare – examples of repurposed cannon being used for street furniture, notably on Bankside, and an upside down one beside St Helen's Bishopsgate in the City. So, the design for bollards might have taken inspiration from an upturned cannon with a ball in the muzzle, but the vast majority of cast-iron street bollards were made for the specific purpose of guarding pedestrianized pavements from street traffic.

That's not to say they are not interesting, though! Often bollards are stamped with their location, sometimes the historic parish, and might even be highly decorative, such as some that are found in the City of London.

Streetlights

The first instances of illuminating London's streets can be attributed to Henry Barton, Lord Mayor of the City of London 1416–17 (then again in 1428). It is said he instructed lit lanterns to be hung out from Hallowtide til Candlemas (November to February) although there is no confirmed record of this.

More concrete rules appear with an Act of Parliament in 1766, which introduced regulations for the cleaning, paving and lighting of London's streets. The only resources available for light at this time were flaming torches, and evidence of this can be seen in snuffers that can sometimes be found outside the wealthier homes in London's aristocratic neighbourhoods. Snuffers are cone-shaped protrusions that flank the front door of a house, allowing servants to extinguish their torches after delivering you safely home (see page 70).

The beginnings of modern streetlighting arrived with Friedrich Albrecht Winzer (anglicized to Frederick Albert Winsor). In 1807 he gave the world's first demonstration of

gas-powered streetlighting along Pall Mall and, in 1810, the Gas, Light and Coke Company was officially formed when Winsor received a royal charter from King George IV (r. 1820–30).

In 1986 this became what's known today as British Gas and, though the majority of streetlights are now electric, there are still 1,500 gas lamps across London that are maintained by British Gas. A team of four lamp lighters visit each lamp, using a ladder to climb up and set the times at which the lamp should switch on and off. This timer lasts 14 days and then needs to be reset.

Lampposts

Just like bollards, lampposts can help give you a sense of place in London. In the West End you will find some depicting Saint Martin of Tours, namesake of St Martin-in-the-Fields in Trafalgar Square, and a 4th-century French bishop who is shown giving his cloak to a beggar. All over Westminster you will find a golden swirly 'W' for Westminster and then what appears to be the symbol for Coco Chanel. Although

Above (top) Lighting one of London's gas lamps; **(bottom)** City Council lamppost

it is true that the 2nd Duke of Westminster had an affair with Coco, it is not true that he designed these as a grand romantic gesture. The two 'C's simply stand for City Council.

For the most elaborate lampposts, head to the River Thames. As part of the 19th-century overhaul of London's sewer system, a new public walkway was created alongside the river. This needed some accompanying street furniture and the chosen designs were by George Vulliamy, who had supposedly been inspired by the entwined dolphins on the Fountain of Neptune from Piazza del Popolo in Rome. Installed from 1870, they first appeared on the Victoria Embankment and were then mirrored on the south side of the river on the Albert Embankment, an area that has since become known as the Dolphin Zone, despite the fact that some argue the figures bear a closer resemblance to sturgeon fish. Two further designs that didn't make the cut can be found on Chelsea Embankment – a lion's paw design by Joseph Bazalgette, and the two boys clambering up

Above Coalbrookdale lamppost
Opposite (top) St Martin-in-the-Fields lamppost; **(bottom)** Swan bench

the thicker lamppost, designed by Timothy Butler for the Coalbrookdale Company. Replica dolphin lampposts have been created throughout the 20th century so now you can see them lining most of the river in Central London.

Benches

Alongside lampposts, George Vulliamy also designed benches for the Victoria Embankment between 1872 and 1874. But instead of Rome, this time he looked to Egypt for inspiration and his benches are flanked either by camels or sphinxes. Vulliamy, who had visited Egypt, also designed the pair of sphinx and pedestal for Cleopatra's Needle which arrived in 1878.

On the south side of the Thames, along Albert Embankment, there are more animal-themed cast-iron benches – this time depicting swans. Although these were also installed in the 1800s, are grade II listed and within Lambeth's conservation area, it is not confirmed whether these were also designed by Vulliamy.

Essential information

Getting to London

London is served by six international airports, but the main central ones are London City, London Gatwick and London Heathrow. From each of these, there are direct rail or London Underground services into Central London. You can also take a taxi. For more thorough information, relevant to your location, visit *visitlondon.com/traveller-information/travel-to-london*

Getting around London

London is well served by public transport and it is almost part of the experience to use the London Underground or a Routemaster bus. You might find it helpful to check online using TFLs Journey Planner (*tfl.gov.uk/plan-a-journey*) or to download an app such as TFL Go or (my favourite) CityMapper to help decide on the best routes. The latter presents you with all the options for travelling across London by Tube, rail and bus, as well as an estimated time and cost for a taxi.

The easiest way to pay for Tube, bus and rail journeys is pay as you go using a contactless card or a smartphone. You are only charged for the journeys you make and there are daily and weekly caps. If your card or mobile has this symbol))) you can use it. You can also use Apple Pay.

Children under the age of 11 travel free with a paying adult on almost all TFL services, check their website (*tfl.gov.uk*) for details. If you are planning to use a taxi, only hail a registered black cab with its distinctive shape. They have their light on when available.

Tips for first-time visitors

Do not eat out in the immediate vicinity of Leicester Square (or in general anywhere where there's someone standing outside trying to usher you in!).

If you are planning a journey in Central London it might be best to walk. The London Underground map can be deceptive about distances, and heavy traffic means it often is the quickest route. Plus it gives you a chance to look up!

Stand on the right on escalators. This is generally only adhered to on the Underground. Walking on pavements, there are no hard-or-fast rules, which leads to a lot of 'excuse me, sorry's.

Avoid rickshaws, they are not licensed or officially regulated and are often unsafe.

Useful websites

My favourite London websites

For things to do as well as food and drink recommendations
- *timeout.com/london/things-to-do*
- *londonist.com/things-to-do*
- *thenudge.com/london-things-to-do*
- *littlelondonwhispers.com*

For history
british-history.ac.uk
A digital library of historic sources including an online version of the Survey of London.

historicengland.org.uk/listing/the-list
Search the register of nationally protected buildings, structures, gardens and monuments.

londonist.com/category/features history
This site is entertaining and thorough as well as occasionally being delightfully opinionated and super niche. See also Matt Brown's (Editor at Large) book *Everything you Know About London is Wrong*.

ianvisits.co.uk
A fantastic blog on London's history and geeky details – especially good for quirky events and Tube/rail updates.

ghostsigns.co.uk
Sam is the absolute authority on ghost signs (and his book on the subject, *Ghost Signs, A London Story*, is fantastic!).

londonremembers.com
Undertaking the impressive task of recording all London plaques and memorials.

layersoflondon.org/map
View and overlay historic maps of London.

Map links
You can find links to a Google Map of all 10 featured walks on my website. Each walk has the route and stops plotted for you to follow in real time on your phone. You'll find them at *lookup.london/book-walk-maps*.

Also on my website, you can sign up to my weekly newsletter, sharing a new blog post about a bit of London's hidden history every Wednesday morning.

Index

Page numbers in *italics* indicate illustration captions.

A note on sources

I'm not an academic historian and I think that the role of a historian is different to that of a tour guide or history blogger.

However it's always been very important to me to understand and convey the truth of a story rather than just repeat urban myths, accepted truths or lazy assumptions.

Among my ever-expanding collection of London history books, I'm constantly referring back to Pevsner's architectural guides when I first spot a detail. I also rely on British History Online, Historic England's National Heritage List, online planning documents, old maps and a number of fellow dedicated London history bloggers (see page 216) to cross-reference historic facts and wheedle out my favourite stories.

Picture credits

All images supplied by the author, with the following exceptions:

About the author

Katie Wignall is the founder of Look Up London – a multi award-winning London history blog and walking tour company. She runs public walks and private tours across London, specializing in the more unusual history of the city and sites off the beaten track. Her walks are regularly ranked #1 among more than 1,500 tours in London on Tripadvisor. Katie grew up (and still lives) in southwest London. She qualified as a London Blue Badge Tourist Guide in 2018 and an official City of London Guide in 2021. She is also the author of *Abandoned London* by Amber Books Limited. You can find out more at www.lookup.london and follow Katie on Twitter and Instagram @look_uplondon, tiktok @lookuplondon and Facebook @lookuplondonwalks.

First published in Great Britain in 2022 by Greenfinch
An imprint of Quercus Editions Ltd
Carmelite House
50 Victoria Embankment
London
EC4Y 0DZ

An Hachette UK company

A CIP catalogue record for this book is available from the British Library

PB ISBN 978-1-52941-942-9

eBook ISBN 978-1-52941-943-6

10 9 8 7 6 5 4 3 2

Design by Sarah Pyke

Illustrated maps: Laura Barnard

Printed and bound in China

MIX
Paper from
responsible sources
FSC® C104740

Papers used by Greenfinch are from well-managed
forests and other responsible sources.